Sweet and deliciou... y chefs

James MacDougall

Formac Publishing Company Limited
Halifax, Nova Scotia

Formac Publishing Company Limited acknowledges the support of the Culture Division, Nova Scotia Department of Tourism, Culture and Heritage. We acknowledge the financial support of the Government of Canada through the Book Publishing Industry Development Program (BPIDP) for our publishing activities.
We acknowledge the support of the Canada Council for the Arts for our publishing program.

The Canada Council | Le Conseil des Arts
for the Arts | du Canada

ONTARIO ARTS COUNCIL
CONSEIL DES ARTS DE L'ONTARIO

Library and Archives Canada Cataloguing in Publication

MacDougall, James, 1966-
        Patisseries : recipes from Canada's best chefs / James MacDougall.

Includes index.
ISBN 10: 0-88780-678-3
ISBN 13: 978-0-88780-678-0

        1. Pastry.   2. Confectionery.   I. Title.

TX765.M32 2005   641.8'65   C2005-904530-2

Formac Publishing Company Limited
5502 Atlantic Street
Halifax, Nova Scotia B3H 1G4
www.formac.ca

Printed and bound in Canada

Photo credits:

Perry Jackson: 1, 5, 6, (top right, bottom left), 9, 11, 13, 14, 17, 19, 23, 27, 33, 34 (top right, bottom left), 40, 44, 47, 53, 54, 59, 60, 63, 65, 66 (top right, bottom left), 70, 73, 74, 85, 89

Meghan Collins: 3, 15, 20, 21, 24, 25, 29, 31, 34 (bottom right, top left), 36, 39, 41, 45, 46, 48, 49, 52, 55, 62, 66 (bottom right), 71, 77, 81, 82, 93

Vincenzo Pietropaolo: 6 (top left), 38, 42, 50 (bottom right, bottom left, top left), 58, 78, 79, 80, 86, 90

Lyle Stafford: 6 (bottom right), 28, 43, 50 (top right), 57, 66 (top left), 68

Acknowledgement:

The author and publisher acknowledge the following in assisting in the production of this book: Mills Brothers, Halifax, Paderno Factory Store, Halifax.

Contents

Introduction

Patisserie shops and boulangeries are found in many cities across Canada. Like those found all over France, Italy and Germany, they serve a variety of confections, each one having its own character and specialty, according to the owner's passion and skill.

The recipes in this book were gathered from expert pastry chefs. Their generosity of spirit in sharing their secrets has resulted in a profusion of tempting dishes. The collection is as diverse as the featured restaurants, cafés and chocolatiers. Each one is unique, and each one brings out the culture of its own cuisine. Some, like La Have Bakery in Nova Scotia, sell whole grain breads, while Clafouti, in Toronto, features a delicious French fruit dessert of the same name. At Gingerbread Haus in Halifax, the chef highlights German cakes.

Regional ingredients are also significant. These include apples from the Annapolis Valley, cloudberries from Newfoundland and blueberries from British Columbia. Naturally, chefs like to explore new flavours and new ideas. They blend and fuse ingredients, producing exotic combinations in recipes such as milk chocolate chai-spice tarts and Kaffir lime, ginger and coconut custards with lemongrass sorbet.

Baking is a very rewarding craft. The results are beautiful and mouth-watering. It is also a fairly exact science. The balance of wet and dry ingredients is very important. The amount of time the egg yolks are beaten, so that they double or triple in volume, and the careful tempering of chocolate cannot be rushed. It requires patience and precision, and an artist's hand to bring about the best results. It is also useful to understand how the weather, especially humidity, affects the ingredients and can compromise the results. Meringues, for example, are adversely affected by heat and humidity.

These recipes have all been tested and adapted for home cooking and the ingredients are available in most supermarkets. When purchasing ingredients, it is advisable to look for the best quality. While all-purpose flour is a good choice, some recipes really need the fine quality of cake and pastry flour. This soft flour is low in protein and high in starch and is whiter in colour due to a chlorination process that softens the strength of the gluten. Because it contains less of the proteins that produce gluten, it produces a lighter and more crumbly texture, which is preferable in sponge cakes and other light baked goods.

Eggs are the second most important ingredient in baking. The recipes in this book are all based on large eggs, which weigh two ounces: 1 ounce (30 g) being the white, ⅔ ounce (20 g) being the yolk and ⅙ ounce (5 g) the shell. If you do not use large eggs, the measurements of the other ingredients will have to be adjusted.

Butter is also a very important component in the baking process. The recipes in this book are based on unsalted butter, also known as sweet butter. By using unsalted butter one can control the amount of salt in a recipe.

In baking it is very important that these three ingredients are used at room temperature, unless otherwise specified in the recipe.

Another key ingredient in these recipes is chocolate. Although everyone has their personal favourites, it is important to know that chocolate which does not contain cocoa butter is not recommended for these recipes. For best results, one should use chocolate that has at least 20% cocoa butter in its composition. Dark or semi-sweet chocolate is the combination of finely ground cocoa solids with the addition of sugar, vanilla and cocoa butter. Light or milk chocolate has milk powder added to it and contains a maximum of 50% sugar. White chocolate is not a true chocolate because it contains no cocoa solids. It is composed of cocoa butter, milk powder, vanilla, and 55% sugar. These products are found in both the baking and confectionary sections of most supermarkets.

There are two types of unsweetened cocoa powder: natural cocoa powder is untreated, has a slightly acidic taste and is generally light in colour; Dutch processed cocoa powder has been alkalized and will not react with acids, such as baking soda. If a recipe calls for non-alkalized cocoa powder, and Dutch processed cocoa is used, you should omit the baking soda and double the baking powder.

If your local supermarket doesn't carry an ingredient you need, there are many specialty shops that cater to the public. The chef at your favourite restaurant or patisserie would also be a good source of information.

The gathering of these recipes has taken almost two years. Although some of these establishments no longer serve these dishes, we wanted to acknowledge the source of each delicious dessert, and we hope you will discover these cafés, restaurants and specialty stores across Canada.

And for that homemade flavour, we hope you will indulge your family and guests with all these outstanding recipes.

James MacDougall
September 2005
Halifax, N.S.

Cakes

There is no confection more closely associated with celebrations than cakes. The recipes in this section include succulent sponge cakes, as well as richly flavoured tortes and cheesecakes. They include European favourites — Bienen Stich from Germany and Scandinavian Apple Cake — and new culinary delights, such as Banana Whiskey Cake and Roasted Sweet Potato Cheesecake with Gingersnap Crust.

La Cave's Cheesecake

La Cave, Halifax, NS

This is the recipe that made La Cave famous for its cheesecake.

Graham wafer crumb base
1 cup (250 mL) graham wafer crumbs
1 tbsp (15 mL) granulated sugar
1½ tsp (7 mL) melted butter

Filling
1 cup (250 mL) granulated sugar
1 lb (455 g) cream cheese
1 whole egg + 1 egg yolk
½ cup (125 mL) whole milk (3.25%)
½ cup (125 mL) heavy cream (35%)
½ tbsp (7 mL) lemon juice
1 tbsp (15 mL) vanilla

Preheat oven to 215°F (100°C).

In a small bowl, mix all the ingredients for the crust and lightly press into the bottom of a 10-inch (25 cm) springform pan.

In the bowl of an upright mixer fitted with the paddle attachment, cream the sugar and cream cheese together. Add egg and yolk while the mixer is on low speed. Slowly pour milk and cream into the batter to avoid any lumps of cheese. Add lemon juice and vanilla. Pour into the prepared pan and tap lightly on counter to remove any pockets of air in the batter.

Place a pan of boiling water on the bottom rack of oven to add moisture while baking to help prevent cracks from forming on the top of cake. Bake for 90 minutes.

Remove from oven and let cool on wire rack. Refrigerate overnight.

Serve with blueberry sauce (recipe follows).

Blueberry Sauce
6 cups (1500 mL) blueberries
1 cup (250 mL) granulated sugar
¼ cup (65 mL) cornstarch

To make the blueberry sauce, toss the blueberries with the cornstarch and place in a heavy-bottomed saucepan with the sugar. Cook the mixture over medium-high heat until the skins of the berries burst and the sauce thickens slightly. Let the sauce cool and pour it over the top of the cheesecake. Cut the cake into 12 pieces and serve with whipped cream.

Banana Whiskey Cake

Elegant Epicure, London, ON

This cake and pastry cream can be prepared a day ahead of serving.

Banana sponge
6 large eggs, separated
1¼ cups (315 mL) granulated sugar
1½ cups (375 mL) all-purpose flour
1¾ tsp (7.5 mL) baking powder
1 large very ripe banana, mashed
2 tbsp (30 mL) lemon juice
¼ cup (60 mL) cold water
¾ cup (185 mL) granulated sugar

Chocolate butter cream
1¼ cups (315 mL) granulated sugar
¼ cup (60 mL) water
¾ cup (185 mL) light corn syrup
7 large egg yolks
1¼ cups (315 mL) unsalted butter at room
   temperature
1 oz (30 g) semi-sweet chocolate, chopped and
   melted

Pastry cream
¾ cup (185 mL) whole milk (3.25%)
1 large egg
¼ cup (60 mL) granulated sugar
2 tbsp (30 mL) cornstarch
1 tsp (5 mL) vanilla extract

Chocolate ganache
⅔ cup (170 mL) heavy cream (35%)
7 oz (210 g) semi-sweet chocolate, chopped

Kahlua Soak
1 tbsp (15 mL) Kahlua
1 tbsp (15 mL) Irish whiskey
1 cup (250 mL) simple syrup

Preheat oven to 350°F (180°C). Generously grease and flour a 10-inch (25 cm) springform pan.

In the bowl of an electric mixer fitted with the whisk attachment, whip egg yolks with 1¼ cups (315 mL) sugar until it has tripled in volume. Sift in flour and baking powder.

Mix mashed bananas with lemon juice and water. Add to the egg yolk mixture and gently stir until just combined.

In a clean, grease-free bowl, beat egg whites, adding ¾ cup (185 mL) sugar, a little at a time until firm peaks are reached.

Cut and fold the egg whites into the batter in three batches, taking care not to lose volume. Pour into prepared pan and bake for 40-45 minutes. Let cool in pan for 10 minutes. Release the pan, and turn the cake upside down on the base of the pan until completely cooled.

To make the chocolate butter cream, place sugar, water and corn syrup in a medium-sized non-reactive pot, and heat over medium until the sugar has dissolved. Turn heat to high and continue to cook until a candy thermometer reads 300°F (115°C).

While the syrup is coming to temperature, place egg yolks in the bowl of an upright mixer and whisk on high speed until tripled in volume.

At this point, the syrup should be ready. Quickly and carefully, begin to pour the syrup down the side of the bowl as the mixer is going. Continue to whisk at medium speed until cool, about room temperature.

On low speed, begin to add the softened butter by tablespoons until it is all incorporated. Add the melted chocolate and continue to mix until well blended. Cover with plastic wrap until required.

To make the pastry cream, bring milk to a boil. In a medium bowl, whisk together egg, sugar and cornstarch, then slowly pour a little of the hot milk into the egg mixture, stir and pour back into the pot. Over medium-high heat, stir the mixture until thick, like custard.

Remove from heat and add vanilla. Cover with plastic wrap directly on the surface to prevent a skin from forming. Cool and set aside until required.

For the chocolate ganache, heat cream until it just begins to boil. Remove from the heat and add the chocolate. Stir until smooth. Set aside but still keep warm.

For the Kahlua soak, mix all ingredients together.

To assemble, cut the cake into three layers and brush each with the Kahlua soak. With the springform pan back together, cover the top layer of the cake with half of the pastry cream and place in the pan. Cover the middle layer with remaining pastry cream and place on top of the first layer. Place the last layer on top — cut side down — and chill well. Spread a layer of butter cream over the top and sides of the cake and chill again. Pour the ganache over the top of the cake and swirl with a palate knife to have the ganache run and cover the sides of the cake. Chill until the ganache is set.

Roasted Sweet Potato Cheesecake with Gingersnap Crust

Braywick Bistro, London, ON

This ginger-spiced cheesecake takes on a special dimension with the sweet potato purée.

Crust
1 cup (250 mL) gingersnap crumbs
4 tbsp (60 mL) unsalted butter, melted
½ tsp (2 mL) ground ginger
¼ tsp (1 mL) ground cinnamon
¼ tsp (1 mL) ground nutmeg

Filling
2 cups (500 mL) soft cream cheese
½ cup (125 mL) granulated sugar
2 large eggs
¾ tsp (4 mL) ground cinnamon
¼ tsp (1 mL) ground cloves
¼ tsp (1 mL) ground allspice
¼ tsp (1 mL) ground nutmeg
1 cup (250 mL) puréed sweet potato

Garnish (optional)
candied ginger

Preheat oven to 325°F (160°C).

In a small bowl, combine all ingredients for the crust and mix well. Press the crumb mixture firmly into the base of a 10-inch (25 cm) springform pan and a quarter way up the sides. Set aside.

In the bowl of an upright mixer fitted with the paddle attachment, beat the cream cheese and sugar until well combined on low speed. Add eggs one at a time and incorporate well. Mix in spices and sweet potato.

Pour batter into prepared pan, and tap the pan on counter to remove any air pockets that may be in the batter.

Place a pan of boiling water on the bottom rack of oven to add moisture. This helps to prevent cracks in the top of the cheesecake. Bake for 40-50 minutes, or until the sides are firm and the centre is a little soft. Remove from oven and cool on a wire rack. Refrigerate overnight to set firmly.

Cut into 12 pieces and garnish with whipped cream and candied ginger.

Deep Chocolate Torte

Vienna Home Bakery, Toronto, ON

This flourless chocolate torte is just the answer for a gluten-free dessert.

1 lb (455 g) semi-sweet chocolate.
6 large eggs, separated
¼ cup (60 mL) granulated sugar
¾ cup (185 mL) heavy cream (35%)
2 tbsp (30 mL) orange-flavoured liqueur
non-alkalized cocoa powder

Preheat oven to 275°F (125°C) and line a 9-inch (23 cm) springform pan with parchment paper.

Place the chocolate in a medium-sized bowl and set over a pot of simmering water until the chocolate is melted. Remove the bowl, and set aside to cool, until tepid.

In the bowl of an electric mixer fitted with the whip attachment, beat the egg whites and sugar until soft peaks, and transfer them to a clean bowl. Now beat the cream to soft peaks, incorporating the liqueur; transfer to a clean bowl. Whip the egg yolks to the ribbon stage, or until tripled in volume.

Cut and fold the whipped cream into the egg yolks, then fold this mixture into the egg whites, followed by the melted chocolate. Pour the batter into the prepared pan and bake for 40 minutes. The cake should be well risen at this point.

Remove the pan from the oven and allow to cool on a wire rack. The cake will fall gently once removed from the oven. When the cake has cooled to room temperature, remove from the pan. Dust the top with cocoa powder.

Cut the cake into 12 pieces and serve with a dollop of crème fraîche.

Scandinavian Apple Cake

Seven Restaurant & Wine Bar, Halifax, NS

This is a delicious treat in autumn, when freshly picked apples are abundant.

¾ cup (185 mL) melted butter
1 cup (250 mL) granulated sugar
2 large eggs
2 tsp (10 mL) vanilla
2 tsp (10 mL) baking soda
2 tsp (10 mL) baking powder
2 tsp (10 mL) ground cinnamon
2 tsp (10 mL) allspice
1½ tsp (7 mL) ground cardamom
½ tsp (2 mL) salt
2¼ cups (565 mL) all-purpose flour
5 apples, peeled, cored, and chopped

Preheat oven to 350°F (180°C).

Grease and line the bottom of a 10-inch (25 cm) springform pan.

In a large bowl, cream the butter and sugar until light in colour. Mix in eggs one at a time and add vanilla.

Sift in dry ingredients, and mix until blended. Then fold in the apples. Pour into prepared pan and bake for 50-65 minutes.

Remove pan from oven and let cool for 15 minutes on a wire rack.

Let cool completely or serve warm with a dollop of whipped cream.

Colossal Carrot Cake

Cheesecake Café, Calgary, AB

This is a moist and flavourful carrot cake — a sneaky way to get all the goodness of carrots.

Cake

1¾ cups (440 mL) all-purpose flour
1 cup (250 mL) granulated sugar
1¼ tsp (6 mL) baking soda
2¼ tsp (11 mL) baking powder
½ tsp (2 mL) cinnamon
½ tsp (2 mL) allspice
1 tsp (5 mL) nutmeg
½ cup (125 mL) pecan pieces
½ cup (125 mL) shredded coconut
1½ cups (375 mL) grated carrots
⅔ cup (165 mL) drained crushed pineapple
3 eggs
¾ cup (185 mL) buttermilk
⅔ cup (165 mL) vegetable oil

Cream cheese icing

4 8-oz packages (1.2 kg) cream cheese
2 cups (500 mL) icing sugar
¼ cup (60 mL) whole milk
¼ cup (60 mL) lemon juice

Preheat oven to 350°F (180°C).

Grease and line a 10-inch (25 cm) cake pan.

In a large bowl, mix all dry ingredients including pecans, coconut and carrots, using a rubber spatula. Mix well, covering carrots with flour. This will help keep the carrots from sinking to the bottom during baking. Add pineapple and mix until just incorporated.

In a separate bowl, beat together eggs, buttermilk and oil.

Add wet ingredients and mix until just combined.

Pour into prepared pan and bake for one hour in the middle of the oven. This is a very moist cake, so use the touch method for doneness. A cake tester should come out with crumbs still attached.

Remove cake from oven and let cool in pan on wire rack for 15 minutes. Remove from pan and invert.

For the icing, combine all ingredients in an electric mixer until completely incorporated.

Once the cake is completely cooled, cut into three layers. (It may be easier to slightly freeze the cake before doing so.) Layer the cake, alternating with cream cheese icing, finally covering the cake all over with icing.

Hot Chocolate Cakes

Bianca's, St John's, NL

It's a good idea to make the ice cream that accompanies these tasty cakes one to two days ahead.

Cakes
½ cup (125 mL) cocoa powder
8 oz (240 g) semi-sweet chocolate
1 cup (250 mL) unsalted butter
4 whole eggs
4 egg yolks
¼ cup (60 mL) granulated sugar
1 seed of vanilla bean
½ tbsp (7 mL) all-purpose flour
⅛ tsp salt

Ice cream
4 cups (1 L) whole milk (3.25%)
1 cup (250 mL) heavy cream (35%)
1 vanilla bean, split
12 egg yolks
1 cup (250 mL) granulated sugar

Espresso sauce
1 cup (250 mL) heavy cream (35%)
¼ cup (60 mL) ground espresso beans
2 oz (60 g) semi-sweet chocolate
4 tbsp (60 mL) granulated sugar
½ cup (125 mL) whole milk (3.25%)
4 egg yolks

Preheat oven to 350°F (180°C). Generously butter and dust with cocoa powder 8 6-oz (190 mL) ramekins.

In the top of a double boiler, over simmering water, melt the chocolate and butter, stirring constantly to avoid burning. Remove from pot and let cool slightly.

As the chocolate cools, whip eggs, yolks and sugar until the volume has increased by four times. Add vanilla seed to the chocolate mixture. Stir ⅓ of the egg mixture into the chocolate. Gently cut and fold the remaining egg mixture, flour and salt into the chocolate, taking care not to lose too much volume in the eggs.

Pour the batter into prepared ramekins. Place on a sheet pan and bake for 10-12 minutes.

For the ice cream, in a medium-sized saucepan, bring milk, cream and vanilla bean to a boil. As the milk is heating, place the egg yolks and sugar in a large bowl and whisk until pale in colour. When the milk comes to a boil, remove from heat and slowly pour about a cup into the yolks, whisking as you pour to temper the eggs. Pour the yolk mixture back into the pot and constantly stir over medium-high heat until slightly thickened. Remove from heat and let cool. Cover with plastic wrap and refrigerate overnight. Place in ice cream maker and follow the manufacturer's directions. If you do not have an ice cream maker, you can place the custard in the freezer and whisk every 2-3 hours until the ice cream is smooth and well frozen.

To make the espresso sauce, heat the cream, milk, coffee, chocolate and half of the sugar in a medium-sized saucepan until scalded. Remove from heat and let steep for 10 minutes.

In a medium-sized bowl, whisk egg yolks and remaining sugar until pale in colour. Stir in the chocolate cream mixture, and return to the pot. Stir constantly over medium heat until slightly thickened. Remove from heat and allow to cool. Keep refrigerated.

To present the dessert, place a warm cake in the centre of each serving plate. Spoon sauce around cake and top with a scoop of ice cream.

Pumpkin Spice Cake with Maple Glaze

Thyme and Again Creative Catering, Ottawa, ON

The mellow flavour of this maple glaze adds a well-balanced sweetness to the spices of this cake.

Cake

1 cup (250 mL) butter
3 cups (750 mL) granulated sugar
4 eggs
2 cups (500 mL) pumpkin purée
1 cup (250 mL) whole milk (3.25%)
3⅓ cups (830 mL) all-purpose flour
2 tsp (10 mL) cinnamon
½ tsp (2 mL) nutmeg
½ tsp (2 mL) allspice
1 tsp (5 mL) salt
1 tsp (5 mL) baking powder
1 tsp (5 mL) baking soda

Glaze

¾ cup (185 mL) butter
⅓ cup (90 mL) heavy cream (35%)
⅓ cup (90 mL) maple syrup
2 cups (500 mL) icing sugar

Preheat oven to 350°F (180°C).

Grease and flour a 9½-inch (25 cm) cake pan.

In the bowl of an electric mixer fitted with the paddle, cream the butter and sugar until light and fluffy. Add eggs one at a time, making sure each one is well incorporated before adding the next egg.

In separate bowls, sift dry ingredients together, and the pumpkin purée and milk together.

With the mixer on low speed, add ⅓ of dry ingredients, followed by ⅓ of the purée milk mixture. Continue to alternate wet and dry until mixtures are just combined.

Pour batter into prepared pan and bake for 45-50 minutes, or until a cake tester comes out clean.

Remove from oven and cool on a wire rack.

In a medium-sized saucepan, bring the butter, cream and maple syrup to a boil. Stir in icing sugar, and then strain through a metal sieve into a bowl to remove any lumps. Cool in refrigerator.

When both the cake and glaze have cooled, pour the glaze over top of the cake.

Chocolate Cupcakes with Mocha Icing

Cupcake Shoppe, Toronto, ON

The cupcake has returned from near oblivion. These delights are quick to make and can be dressed up and turned into a formal dessert.

Cupcakes

1 cup (250 mL) Dutch cocoa powder
2 cups (500 mL) boiling water
2¾ cups (690 mL) all-purpose flour
½ tsp (2 mL) baking powder
2 tsp (10 mL) baking soda
½ tsp (2 mL) salt
1 cup (250 mL) butter
2½ cup (625 mL) granulated sugar
4 eggs
1½ tsp (7 mL) vanilla

Mocha icing

¼ cup (60 mL) butter
¼ cup (60 mL) strong coffee
2 oz (60 g) baker's chocolate
2¼ cups (565 mL) sifted icing sugar
1 tsp (5 mL) vanilla

Preheat oven to 350°F (180°C).

Line a muffin pan with paper liners.

In a medium-sized bowl, mix cocoa and water together until smooth.

In a second bowl, stir flour, baking powder, baking soda and salt together.

In the bowl of an electric mixer, cream the butter and sugar until light and fluffy. Add eggs one at a time followed by vanilla.

On low speed, add half of the flour mixture. Pour in the cocoa mixture, then the remaining half of the flour, until just mixed.

Fill liners ¾ full and bake for 25-30 minutes.

Remove from oven and cool on a wire rack.

In a medium-sized saucepan, gently heat the butter and coffee. Add the chocolate and melt. Remove from heat and stir in icing sugar and vanilla.

When the cupcakes have cooled completely, spread a thick layer of icing on each.

Summary Cake

Café Europa, London, ON

This taste of summer can be made with any seasonal fruit; substitute your favourite berries.

Biscuit base
3 large eggs, separated
3 tbsp (45 mL) granulated sugar
3 tbsp (45 mL) all-purpose flour

Fruit filling
3 cups (750 mL) fresh strawberries
3½ cups (400 mL) strawberry flavoured juice
5-oz (150 g) package vanilla pudding powder

Filling
4½ cups (1 L) heavy cream
18 oz (540 g) cream cheese
½ cup (125 mL) granulated sugar
2 tsp (10 mL) vanilla sugar
¾ cup (185 mL) sour cream
zest of one orange
3 envelopes of gelatin powder

Topping (optional)
1 cup (250 mL) strawberry juice
2 tsp (10 mL) glaze powder

Garnish
Shredded coconut

Preheat oven to 425°F (220°C).

In a medium-sized bowl, beat egg whites while slowly adding the sugar. Once the sugar has been incorporated, add the egg yolks one at a time followed by the flour. Mix until smooth and press in the bottom of a 10-inch (25 cm) springform pan.

Bake for 10 minutes or until just golden brown. Remove from oven.

In a medium-sized saucepan, cook the strawberries in 3 cups (750 mL) of the juice. When the fruit begins to boil, stir the powdered pudding into the remaining ½ cup (125 mL) of juice, and add to the pot of fruit. Mix well and bring back to boil. Pour the hot mixture over the biscuit base, spread evenly, and allow to cool.

To make the filling, place the heavy cream in the bowl of an electric mixer and whip until firm. Remove from bowl and set aside. In the same mixing bowl, beat the cream cheese, sugar and vanilla sugar until smooth. Add the sour cream and orange zest. Continue to mix until just combined. Set aside.

Dissolve the gelatin in ¼ cup (60 mL) cold water in a small pan. Once the gelatin absorbs the water, gently warm it just until it becomes liquid.

Scrape down the sides of the mixing bowl and add the whipped cream. Continue to mix until just combined. With the mixer on, slowly pour the liquid gelatin into the cheese cream mixture.

Once the filling is well mixed, pour it over the cooled fruit filling. Place in the refrigerator to set, about 4 hours. To glaze the cake, bring the juice and glaze powder to a boil. Let cool until tepid. Pour over top of the cake and sprinkle with shredded coconut.

Flourless Chocolate Cake

Patisserie du Soleil, Calgary, AB

This intensely rich chocolate cake is great for gluten-free decadence.

4½ tbsp (70 mL) cornstarch
6 tbsp (90 mL) cocoa powder
9 egg whites
1 cup (250 mL) granulated sugar
14 egg yolks
2½ oz (70 g) semi-sweet chocolate, melted
2 tbsp (30 mL) espresso or very strong coffee

Preheat oven to 375°F (190°C).

Generously grease a 10-inch (25 cm) springform pan. Sift cornstarch and cocoa together.

In the bowl of an electric mixer, make a meringue with egg whites and sugar. Mix until stiff peaks form. Add egg yolks and combine. Fold the dry ingredients into the meringue. When the cocoa and cornstarch are almost combined, add the melted chocolate and espresso coffee, and continue to mix until just combined.

Pour the batter into the prepared cake pan. Place in the oven and bake for 12-15 minutes. Remove the cake from the oven and let cool on a wire rack.

To serve, place a slice on the centre of the plate, spoon a little crème anglaise around it, and add a scoop of pistachio gelato.

La Ciccolina Chocolate Pâté

Elegant Epicure, London, ON

Serve this dessert with raspberry or other fresh fruit coulis for an exquisite chocolate treat.

1 white pound cake

Coffee soak
1½ cup (375 mL) espresso or very strong coffee
2 tbsp (30 mL) instant coffee granules
¼ cup (60 mL) dark rum
1 tbsp (15 mL) granulated sugar

Chocolate filling
5 oz (150 g) semi-sweet chocolate
5 large eggs, separated
1 tbsp (15 mL) granulated sugar
1 tsp (5 mL) dark cocoa powder

Coating
7 oz (210 g) semi-sweet chocolate

Line a 9 x 4 x 3-inch (2 L) loaf pan with cling wrap. Cut the pound cake into four ¼-inch (5 mm) slices to line the loaf pan (top, two sides and a middle layer).

Make the coffee soak by mixing all the ingredients together while the coffee is hot. Set aside.

To make the chocolate filling, melt the chocolate in the top of a double boiler over hot water. Remove the chocolate from the heat, and allow to cool until tepid.

In a medium-sized bowl, whisk the egg yolks and sugar until light and pale in colour. Add the cocoa powder and the melted chocolate and whisk to combine.

In the bowl of an electric mixer, whip the egg whites until firm peaks. Gently fold the egg whites into the chocolate mixture and set aside.

With a pastry brush, generously soak the slices of pound cake with the coffee soak. Line the bottom and sides of the prepared loaf pan with cake slices. Pour half of the filling into the pan and spread evenly with a rubber spatula. Place the middle layer of soaked pound cake onto the filling, pressing lightly. Pour in the remaining filling, spreading evenly. Cover with cling film and refrigerate overnight to set.

When the cake has set, melt the chocolate, let cool slightly. Remove the cake from the refrigerator, uncover and place on a wire rack. Pour the melted chocolate over the top and sides of the cake, smoothing out with a palate knife. Place the cake back in the refrigerator to let the chocolate harden.

To serve the cake, cut into slices and place on a plate with raspberry coulis and whipped cream.

Lemon Roulade

Happy Baker, Fredericton, NB

Family and friends will love this light lemon cake. It's great for a summer picnic.

Roulade sponge
¼ cup (60 mL) all-purpose flour
1 tbsp (15 mL) cornstarch
4 egg whites
¼ cup (60 mL) granulated sugar
8 egg yolks
2 tsp (10 mL) granulated sugar
pinch of salt
½ lemon, zested

Filling
3 egg yolks
½ cup (125 mL) white wine
½ cup (125 mL) granulated sugar
2 lemons, juiced
zest of one lemon
1 envelope of gelatin powder
½ cup (125 mL) cream (35%), whipped

Preheat oven to 425°F (220°C).

Line a 12 x 16-inch (30 x 40 cm) baking sheet with parchment paper, and spray with baking spray.

In a small bowl, mix flour and cornstarch together and set aside.

In the bowl of an electric mixer, whip the egg whites and ¼ cup (60 mL) sugar, until soft peaks.

In a third bowl, stir yolks, 1 tbsp (15 mL) sugar, salt and lemon zest together. Carefully fold egg whites into the yolk mixture. It is best to do this in three batches as not to deflate the volume of the whites. Sift the flour and cornstarch into the batter and carefully fold until just combined.

Pour the batter onto the prepared pan, spread evenly with a spatula and bake for 7-10 minutes, or until the sponge springs back when lightly touched. When the roulade is baked, remove from the oven and turn out onto a damp towel. Roll on the long side, like a jellyroll. Set aside.

While the sponge is cooling, begin the filling. In a large bowl over a pot of simmering water, whisk yolks, wine, sugar, lemon juice and zest until it is light and fluffy. At this point, the mixture should be about 110°F (45°C). Add gelatin and continue to whisk off the heat until the gelatin has dissolved.

Place the mixture over a bowl of ice and continue to whisk until cooled. Take care not to cool too much, as the gelatin will set. Gently fold the whipped cream into the cooled mixture.

Unroll the sponge and spread the filling over it, leaving about an inch at the sides so the filling does not leak out as you roll the cake.

To roll the cake, lift the towel evenly and keep pulling in an upward motion, trying to keep it as even as possible. When the sponge is rolled, let it set in the refrigerator for about 40 minutes. Dust with icing sugar, slice and serve with a small pool of raspberry purée and whipped cream.

Raspberry Financier Cakes with Vanilla Cream

Senses Bakery, Vancouver, BC

The browned butter, or *beurre noisette*, in this recipe adds a nutty flavour to these little cakes.

Cakes
½ cup (125 mL) unsalted butter
½ cup (125 mL) all-purpose flour
1 cup (250 mL) ground toasted hazelnuts
1 cup (250 mL) icing sugar
4 egg whites
2 tbsp (30 mL) honey
1½ cups (375 mL) fresh raspberries

Vanilla cream
½ vanilla bean
2 tbsp (30 mL) granulated sugar
1 cup (250 mL) whipping cream
2 cups (500 mL) fresh raspberries

Preheat oven to 375°F (190°C).

Lightly grease a 13-inch (27 cm) tart pan or 12 individual 3-inch (7 cm) tartlet pans.

Place butter in small saucepan and gently cook until brown. Let cool.

In a mixing bowl, combine flour, ground hazelnuts and icing sugar. With the mixer on low speed, begin to add egg whites, honey and browned butter. Cover and refrigerate for three hours, or overnight.

Place 3 tbsp (45 mL) of batter into prepared tartlet pan. Place six raspberries on top of each cake, and bake for 15 minutes.

Remove from oven and let cool.

For the vanilla cream, scrape the seeds from the vanilla pod and blend with granulated sugar. In the bowl of an electric mixer, beat the whipping cream. When it reaches soft peaks, add vanilla sugar, and continue to beat until cream holds medium peaks.

Top the cakes with vanilla cream and fresh raspberries.

White Chocolate Cheesecake

Herald Street Café, Victoria, BC

To give cheesecake time to set, prepare and bake one day ahead of serving time.

Crust
½ cup (125 mL) graham wafer crumbs
½ cup (125 mL) butter, melted

Filling
16 oz (455 g) white chocolate, chopped
4 8-oz packages (900 g) cream cheese
2 cups (500 mL) granulated sugar
3 large eggs
½ cup (125 mL) pastry flour
1 cup (250 mL) sour cream

Preheat oven to 250°F (120°C). Line a 10-inch (25 cm) springform pan with parchment paper, bottom and sides.

To make the crust, mix graham wafer crumbs and butter until blended. Pour in the prepared pan and lightly pat. Set aside.

Place the chocolate in a glass bowl and melt in a microwave for about 30 seconds, or until almost melted. Set aside.

In the bowl of an upright mixer fitted with the paddle, begin to mix the cream cheese and sugar on low speed. Add eggs one at a time, making sure each is fully incorporated before adding the next. Sift in flour and mix. Add the sour cream and mix until just combined. Pour in the melted chocolate and combine.

Pour the batter into the prepared pan and bake for 45 minutes. Turn off oven and leave cake in the oven for 1 hour. Remove and let cool to room temperature. Chill in refrigerator overnight.

Bienen Stich

Gingerbread Haus Bakery, Halifax, NS

The name of this cake is German for bee sting —
hence the little 'sting' of honey in the recipe.

Yeast dough
1½ tsp (7 mL) dry active yeast
½ cup (125 mL) whole milk (3.25%), warm
⅛ cup (32 mL) granulated sugar
2 cups (500 mL) all-purpose flour
1 egg yolk
small pinch salt
½ tsp (2 mL) lemon juice

Caramel topping
¼ cup (125 mL) butter
2 tbsp (30 mL) cream (35%)
2 tbsp (30 mL) honey
¼ cup (60 mL) granulated sugar
⅓ cup (90 mL) sliced almonds

Pastry cream
1½ tsp (7 mL) powdered gelatin
2½ tbsp (40 mL) whole milk (3.25%)
1 egg yolk
1 tbsp (15 mL) cornstarch
½ tsp (2 mL) vanilla
1 cup (250 mL) whole milk (3.25%)
¼ cup (60 mL) granulated sugar
1¾ cups (440 mL) whipping cream (35%)
2 tbsp (30 mL) icing sugar

Preheat oven to 350°F (180°C).

In the bowl of an electric mixer, dissolve the yeast in warm milk with the sugar. When the yeast has become bubbly, add the remaining ingredients and begin mixing, with the hook attachment, on low speed. Work the dough until it is smooth. Remove the bowl from the mixer and cover. Place in a warm draft-free area until the dough has doubled in size.

While the dough is rising, begin the caramel topping. In a heavy-bottom saucepan on high heat, bring butter, cream, honey and sugar to a boil. Continue to cook until a deep amber colour is reached. Quickly remove the pan from the heat and stir in almonds. Allow to cool slightly.

When the dough has risen, punch down to remove the air. Roll the dough out to fit a 10-inch (25 cm) springform pan. Cover the top of the dough with the warm caramel topping, and allow to rise until it has tripled in size. Place in the oven and bake until the top is a dark amber colour. Remove from oven and allow to cool completely.

To make the pastry cream, dissolve gelatin in 2½ tbsp (40 mL) milk and set aside. In a medium-sized bowl, mix egg yolk, cornstarch and vanilla together, and set aside. In a saucepan, bring 1 cup of milk and sugar to a boil. Slowly pour the hot milk into the egg mixture while stirring.

Return to pan and stir constantly over medium heat until thick and custard-like. Remove from heat and stir in softened gelatin until well combined. Pour into a bowl and cover with buttered film wrap to prevent a skin from forming on top. Cool completely.

When the pastry cream has cooled, whip the cream and icing sugar together until soft peaks form. Gently fold the cream into the cooled pastry cream.

To assemble, cut the cake into two layers and make 12 equal wedges from the top layer. Cover the bottom of the cake with the pastry cream filling, then place the 12 wedges on top of filling and refrigerate overnight.

To serve the 12 wedges, dust with icing sugar and place a dollop of whipped cream on each piece.

Gingerbread with Caramelized Apples

Prairie Ink Restaurant and Bakery, Saskatoon, SK

Sweet caramelized apples give this gingerbread a pleasant autumnal aroma.

Gingerbread

3 cups (750 mL) granulated sugar
5 cups (1250 mL) all-purpose flour
1 tbsp (15 mL) baking soda
4½ tsp (25 mL) ground ginger
3 tbsp (45 mL) ground cinnamon
¾ tsp (4 mL) ground cloves
¾ tsp (4 mL) salt
1½ cups (375 mL) butter at room temperature
¾ cup (185 mL) large eggs
2¼ cups (560 mL) buttermilk
⅓ cup (85 mL) molasses

Caramelized apples

1½ lbs (680 g) McIntosh apples
1 cup (250 mL) brown sugar, lightly packed
1 tbsp (30 mL) cinnamon
½ cup (125 mL) granulated sugar
¼ cup (60 mL) water
1 cup (250 mL) heavy cream (35%)

Preheat oven to 325°F (160°C). Generously grease an angel food cake pan.

In the bowl of an upright mixer with the paddle attachment, combine sugar, flour, baking soda, spices, salt and butter. Mix until crumbly and pea-size. Add eggs, buttermilk and molasses.

Mix until combined. Pour batter into prepared pan and bake 45-60 minutes, or until a cake tester comes out clean. Allow cake to cool for five minutes, then invert on a cooling rack to remove pan.

As the cake cools, prepare the apples. Peel, core and slice the fruit. Toss them in brown sugar and cinnamon in a bowl. Bake for 20-25 minutes on a pan lined with parchment or waxed paper.

To make the caramel sauce, place sugar and water in a small heavy-bottom saucepan. Allow sugar to dissolve over medium heat. When sugar dissolves, increase heat to high and cook until a dark amber colour. Remove from heat and slowly add cream while whisking. Caution should be taken when doing this as the steam and bubbling of the cream can burn you very easily.

Place gingerbread on serving plate, top with caramelized apple slices and drizzle generously with caramel sauce.

Patisseries, Cookies & Squares

Everyone loves a sweet treat, either as dessert or a mid-afternoon indulgence. The crunchy biscotti and the elegant Empire Belgian Cookies in this section make a great accompaniment at mid-morning coffee break. For a light touch, there are meringues, and for something traditional, there are two variations on chocolate brownies.

Tiramisu

Julien's Bakery and Café, Halifax, NS

Tiramisu is a refreshing Italian dessert. Literally translated it means 'pick-me-up.'

Biscuit cuillère
7 large eggs, separated
1¼ cups (320 mL) granulated sugar
¼ cup (65 mL) all-purpose flour
4½ tbsp (70 mL) cornstarch

Mascarpone mousse
10 large egg yolks
1 cup (250 mL) icing sugar
2 cups (500 mL) mascarpone, room temperature
2 cups (500 mL) heavy cream (35%), whipped
  to soft peaks

Coffee flavouring
1½ cups (375 mL) espresso, cooled

Garnish
cocoa powder

Preheat oven to 450°F (230°C). Line a baking pan with parchment paper.

In the bowl of an electric mixer fitted with the whip attachment, whip 7 egg whites until firm peaks are formed.

In a medium-sized bowl, stir in 4 egg yolks and sugar until combined. Sift flour and cornstarch over the egg mixture. Quickly stir ⅓ of the whipped egg whites into the mixture. Cut and fold the remaining whites in gently.

With a palate knife, spread batter evenly over prepared baking sheet. Bake 10-12 minutes, or until golden and springs back when touched. Remove from oven and let cool on wire rack.

Peel parchment paper from the bottom. Cut into 20 discs about 2½ inches (6 cm) in diameter. Set aside.

To make the mascarpone mousse, whisk egg yolks and sugar together until pale. Whisk in the mascarpone. Cut and fold whipped cream into the mixture. Set aside.

To assemble the tiramisu, prepare 10 small ramekins. Lightly soak 10 cookie discs in the cooled coffee and place in the bottom of the ramekins. Fill the ramekins halfway with mascarpone mousse and place another coffee-soaked cookie disc on top. Fill the ramekins with the remaining mousse. Sprinkle cocoa powder on top. Place in refrigerator to set.

Pistachio-Cranberry Biscotti

Queen of Tarts, Toronto, ON

Biscotti is often served with Vin Santo, a sweet Italian dessert wine, or espresso for dipping.

½ cup (125 mL) unsalted butter
¾ cup (185 mL) granulated sugar
¾ cup (185 mL) brown sugar
½ tsp (2 mL) vanilla extract
zest of 1 orange
1½ tsp (7 mL) ground cinnamon
3 large eggs
3¼ cups (815 mL) all-purpose flour
1 tsp (5 mL) baking powder
½ tsp (2 mL) salt
½ cup (125 mL) pistachios
½ cup (125 mL) dried cranberries

Preheat oven to 350°F (180°C).

In a bowl of an upright electric mixer fitted with the paddle attachment, cream butter, granulated sugar and brown sugar together on medium speed until light and fluffy.

Turn speed on low. Add vanilla, orange zest and cinnamon. Mix until incorporated. Add eggs one at a time, scraping down the sides of the bowl after each egg. Add flour, salt and baking powder. Mix until just combined. Pour in cranberries and pistachios; blend until evenly distributed through dough.

On a lightly floured work surface, turn dough out and divide into three equal pieces. Roll dough into logs about 3 inches (7 cm) in diameter. Place logs approximately 6 inches (15 cm) apart on parchment-lined baking pans. Bake for 45-50 minutes, or until golden in colour and firm to the touch. Remove from the oven.

Cut logs on an angle into ¾ inch (2 cm) slices. Place cut slices back on pan standing up and re-bake for 10 minutes.

Store in an airtight container for up to one month.

Spicy Chocolate Biscotti

Thyme and Again Creative Catering, Ottawa, ON

If you like spice, try adding a little chili powder to this biscotti recipe.

3 large eggs
1 cup (250 mL) granulated sugar
½ tbsp (7 mL) vanilla extract
2 cups (500 mL) all-purpose flour
¼ cup (60 mL) cocoa powder
1 tsp (5 mL) baking powder
½ tsp (2 mL) baking soda
½ tsp (2 mL) ground cinnamon
½ tsp (2 mL) ground allspice
¼ tsp (1 mL) salt
½ tsp (2 mL) ginger powder
½ tsp (2 mL) ground white pepper
1 cup (250 mL) chocolate chips

Preheat oven to 350°F (180°C). Line baking pan with parchment paper.

In the bowl of an electric mixer fitted with the paddle attachment, cream together eggs, sugar and vanilla. Scrape down the sides of the bowl. Add all remaining ingredients, except the chocolate chips, and continue to mix on low speed. Add chocolate chips and combine until evenly distributed through the dough.

Turn dough out onto a lightly floured work surface and divide dough into four equal pieces. Roll dough into logs 3 inches (7 cm) in diameter. Place on baking sheet and bake for 30-35 minutes, or until golden brown and lightly firm to the touch. Remove from oven and let cool slightly. Cut logs on an angle into ¾-inch (2 cm) slices.

Turn oven down to 325°F (160°C). Stand cookie slices up on baking sheet and continue to bake 15 minutes, or until dry. Remove from oven and cool on a wire rack.

Cheesecake Brownies

Room for Dessert, Dundas, ON

These delightful brownies can be cut into heart shapes and glazed with chocolate for that special someone.

4 oz (120 g) semi-sweet chocolate, finely
   chopped
1 cup (250 mL) unsalted butter
2 cups (500 mL) granulated sugar
3 large eggs
1 tsp (5 mL) vanilla extract
1 cup (250 mL) all-purpose flour
½ tsp (2 mL) salt
8-oz (240 g) package cream cheese
½ cup (125 mL) granulated sugar (2nd amount)
1 large egg (2nd amount)

Preheat oven to 325°F (160°C). Line an 8 x 8-inch (20 x 20 cm) square pan with parchment paper or foil wrap extended over the sides by 1 inch (3 cm).

Set a large bowl over a pot of simmering water, melt chocolate and butter together. When chocolate has melted, remove bowl from heat and stir in sugar. Whisk the eggs in one at a time, followed by the vanilla. Stir in flour and salt. Mix until well combined. Pour mixture into prepared pan.

In a medium-sized bowl, beat cream cheese and 2nd amount of sugar together until smooth. Add the egg (2nd amount) and continue to beat until well combined.

Place the cream cheese mixture into a pastry bag fitted with a small plain tip. Pipe lines across the brownie base. With the tip of a small knife, drag through the cheese mixture to create a marble effect. Bake for 20-30 minutes or until batter is set. Remove from oven and cool on a wire rack.

When cooled, remove brownies from the pan by gently lifting the foil wrap that extends over the sides.

Purdy's Nanaimo Bars

Purdy's Chocolates, Vancouver, BC

These Nanaimo bars are an upscale version of a childhood favourite.

Bottom layer
½ cup (125 mL) unsalted butter
¼ cup (60 mL) granulated sugar
1 large egg, beaten
5 tbsp (75 mL) cocoa powder
1¾ cups (440 mL) graham wafer crumbs
½ cup (125 mL) almonds, finely chopped
1 cup (250 mL) unsweetened coconut

Second layer
½ cup (125 mL) unsalted butter
3 tbsp (45 mL) heavy cream (35%)
2 tbsp (30 mL) vanilla custard powder
2 cups (500 mL) icing sugar

Third layer
4 oz (120 g) fine semi-sweet chocolate
2 tbsp (30 mL) unsalted butter

In the top pot of a double boiler, melt butter with sugar. Add the egg and cook until slightly thick.

Remove the pot from the double boiler. Stir in the remaining ingredients until well combined. Press firmly into a 8 x 8-inch (20 x 20 cm) square pan lined with foil extending 2 inches (5 cm) over the sides.

Make the second layer by creaming all the ingredients together with an electric mixer. Mix until light in colour. Spread evenly over the bottom layer. Place in the refrigerator to set slightly.

Set a medium-sized bowl over a pot of simmering water. Melt chocolate and butter together stirring constantly until smooth. Remove the bowl from the pot and let cool slightly. Pour the mixture over the first two layers. Return to the refrigerator to set.

When set, remove squares from pan by lifting on the extended foil wrap. Cut into 2-inch (5 cm) squares.

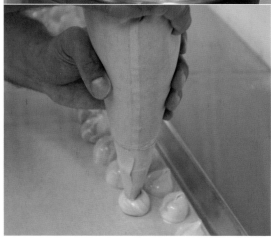

Flavoured Meringues

Fleurdelys Patisserie, Toronto, ON

A spin on the classic fruit fool, the meringues add a pleasant texture to this light dessert, which is great with a glass of sparkling wine.

Meringues
2 cups (500 mL) granulated sugar
1 cup (250 mL) egg whites
½ cup (125 mL) fruit purée

Garnish
1 cup (250 mL) heavy cream (35%)
¼ cup (60 mL) icing sugar
fruit purée

Preheat oven to 200°F (90°C).

Set a medium-sized bowl over simmering water and whisk egg whites and sugar until sugar dissolves.

Pour the mixture into the bowl of a mixer fitted with the whip attachment, and beat on high speed until firm peaks. Fold in fruit purée.

Fill a pastry bag with the mixture. Pipe little balls onto a parchment-lined baking pan. Bake for 2-3 hours or until dry.

Place five or six meringue balls in a large martini glass. Pour fruit purée over top and add a dollop of cream.

Meringue balls can be stored in an airtight container for up to two weeks.

Empire Belgian Cookies

La Baguette et L'Echalote, Vancouver, BC

These buttery, melt-in-your-mouth cookies go well with a tall glass of milk.

2 cups (500 mL) unsalted butter, room
   temperature
1 tbsp (15 mL) vanilla extract
1 cup (250 mL) granulated sugar
4¼ cups (1060 mL) pastry flour
1 tsp (5 mL) baking soda
1 tsp (5 mL) salt
raspberry preserves

Preheat oven to 350°F (180°C).

In a large bowl, cream butter, vanilla and sugar together. Sift in dry ingredients and mix until combined.

Roll dough out to ¼ inch (5 mm) in thickness and cut into circles. Take half of the unbaked cookies and cut the centre out with a smaller cutter. Place cookies on a baking sheet lined with parchment paper and bake for 15 minutes. Remove from oven and let rest on pan for 5 minutes. When cookies have set, move to a wire rack to cool completely.

Place a spoonful of raspberry preserves on the cookie base (no hole) and place a cookie with a hole in it on top. Sprinkle with icing sugar.

Hazelnut Crumble Brownies

With the Grain, Guelph, ON

These brownies are best sandwiched with vanilla almond fudge ice cream and raspberry sauce.

Brownie base
10 tbsp (150 mL) unsalted butter, room temperature
¾ cup (185 mL) granulated sugar
2 large eggs
1 tsp (5 mL) vanilla extract
12 oz (360 g) semi-sweet chocolate, melted
2 cups (500 mL) all-purpose flour

Filling
1 cup (250 mL) raspberry preserves

Crumble topping
1½ cups (375 mL) all-purpose flour
1 cup (250 mL) granulated sugar
10 tbsp (150 mL) unsalted butter
1 orange, zest and juice
¾ cup (185 mL) hazelnut pieces, toasted

Preheat oven to 325°F (160°C).

In the bowl of a mixer fitted with the paddle attachment on low speed, cream together butter and sugar until well combined. Add eggs one at a time and mix well. Add vanilla.

Pour in melted chocolate, followed by the flour. Mix on low speed until all ingredients are combined.

Press the brownie base into a 8 x 8-inch (20 x 20 cm) square pan lined with foil, extending the foil 2 inches (5 cm) over the sides. Bake for 10-12 minutes. The brownies should be a little under-baked. Remove from the oven and cool slightly.

Spread the raspberry preserves evenly over the brownie base.

In a large bowl, mix all ingredients for the crumble topping together with your hands until a crumbly mixture. Spread the crumble mixture over the preserves and place back in the oven for 10-12 minutes, or until the topping is golden brown. Remove from oven and let cool in the pan on a wire rack.

Cut into 2-inch (5 cm) squares.

Oatcakes

LaHave Bakery, LaHave, NS

As wholesome and nutritious as Scottish oatcakes, but a good deal sweeter, these are delicious for breakfast, lunch or a late-night snack.

3 cups (750 mL) rolled oats
2 cups (500 mL) all-purpose flour
1 cup (250 mL) whole wheat flour
½ cup (125 mL) granulated sugar
½ cup (125 mL) brown sugar
1 tsp (5 mL) sea salt
1 tsp (5 mL) baking soda
¾ cup (185 mL) unsalted butter
¾ cup (185 mL) vegetable shortening
⅓ cup (85 mL) water
extra rolled oats for rolling

Preheat oven to 350°F (180°C).

In a large bowl, combine all dry ingredients. Cut in butter and shortening with a pastry blender. Slowly add water, just enough to hold the dough together.

On a large work surface, generously cover dough with the extra rolled oats. Roll the dough to ¼ inch (5 mm) in thickness. Cut into 2 x 4-inch (5 x 10 cm) cakes. Bake on a pan lined with parchment paper for 15-20 minutes.

Turtle Squares

Gleneagle Bakery, Dartmouth, NS

These caramel pecan delights will please even the most discerning sweet tooth.

Base
4½ cups (1120 mL) flour
1½ cups (375 mL) brown sugar
1 cup (250 mL) margarine
1½ cups (375 mL) pecans

Topping
1 cup (250 mL) butter
1 cup (250 mL) margarine
1⅓ cups (330 mL) brown sugar
½ cup (125 mL) light corn syrup
2 cups (500 mL) chocolate chips

Preheat oven to 350°F (180°C).

Line a 9 x 13-inch (20 x 30 cm) square pan with foil extending 2 inches (5 cm) over the sides.

In a large bowl, combine all ingredients for the base until crumbly in texture. Spread evenly over prepared pan. Cover with pecans and press lightly.

In a heavy-bottomed saucepan, combine all ingredients for the topping, except the chocolate chips, and bring to a boil. Cook until thick. Pour over base and bake until bubbly all over the top. Remove from oven and let cool slightly.

Sprinkle chocolate chips over top and spread with a palate knife. Refrigerate until set.

Lift the squares from the pan by gently pulling on the extended foil. Cut into 2-inch (5 cm) squares.

Crispy Meringues with Lemon Curd

Café Brio, Victoria, BC

Nothing says summer like a refreshing lemony dessert, especially when it is accompanied by fresh blackberries.

Meringues
½ cup (125 mL) egg whites
½ tsp (2 mL) cream of tartar
⅓ cup (85 mL) granulated sugar
¼ cup (65 mL) icing sugar

Lemon curd
2 large eggs
4 large egg yolks
½ cup (125 mL) lemon juice
¾ cup (185 mL) granulated sugar
zest of 2 lemons
¼ cup (60 mL) unsalted butter

Stencil
small piece of cardboard with a 3-inch (7 cm)
  square cut from the centre

Garnish
fresh blackberries

Preheat oven to 200°F (90°C).

In the bowl of an upright mixer fitted with the whip attachment, beat egg whites on high until frothy. Add cream of tartar and continue to beat. Slowly pour in the two sugars and whip until stiff peaks.

On a baking sheet lined with parchment paper, make squares of meringue using the stencil. Bake in oven for 2-3 hours or until dry.

In a heavy-bottomed, non-reactive pot over medium heat, whisk eggs, yolks, sugar and lemon juice until thick. Remove from heat. Whisk in butter and zest. Strain into a bowl. Place plastic wrap directly on the surface to avoid a skin from forming. Refrigerate until needed.

To serve, use a little of the lemon curd as glue to stick the first meringue layer to the plate. Cover the layer with lemon curd and continue until three or four meringues high. Garnish with fresh blackberries.

Caramelized Banana Fritters

Braywick Bistro, London, ON

Fritters can be made in advance and frozen in airtight containers for up to two weeks. When ready to serve, re-heat in the oven or in hot oil.

Pâté au choux
1 cup (250 mL) whole milk (3.25%)
¼ cup (60 mL) unsalted butter
pinch of salt
1 tbsp (15 mL) granulated sugar
1 cup (250 mL) all-purpose flour
5 eggs

Caramelized bananas
½ cup (125 mL) butter
½ cup (125 mL) dark brown sugar
6 bananas, sliced
¼ cup (65 mL) dark rum
3 tbsp (45 mL) heavy cream (35%)
8 cups (2 L) frying oil

In a heavy-bottomed pot, bring milk, butter, salt and sugar to a full boil. Add the flour, stirring vigorously until the dough pulls away from the sides of the pot and forms a ball.

Place the dough in an upright mixer fitted with the paddle attachment. Add eggs one at a time, making sure each egg is well absorbed by the dough.

Cut six squares of parchment paper measuring 5 inches x 5 inches (13 cm x 13 cm), and dust with flour.

Place the batter in a piping bag fitted with a large plain tip. Pipe circles on the parchment paper.

In a large saucepan, preheat oil to 350°F (180°C). Slowly slide the batter in. Depending on the size of the pan, cook one or two at a time until golden brown on both sides. Once the paper comes free, remove and discard. Drain the fritters on absorbent towel. Keep warm in oven.

For the caramelized bananas, melt butter and brown sugar in a large non-reactive skillet, over medium-high heat. When butter and sugar begin to caramelize, add the bananas and cook for one minute. Carefully pour in the rum and ignite. When the flames go out, pour in the cream in and swirl until incorporated.

To present, place one fritter in the centre of serving plate and spoon the hot caramelized bananas into the middle of the fritter. Serve with a dollop of whipped cream or ice cream.

Cinnamon Buns

Tall Grass Prairie Bakery, Winnipeg, MB

The aroma of these sweet cinnamon buns is irresistible.

2½ cups (625 mL) warm water
¼ cup (60 mL) brown sugar
1 tbsp (15 mL) dry active yeast
2¾ cups (700 mL) whole wheat flour
4 cups (1L) all-purpose flour
⅓ cup (85 mL) canola oil
1 tbsp (15 mL) salt
1 large egg
1 egg yolk
⅓ cup (85 mL) butter, melted
1 cup (250 mL) brown sugar (2nd amount)
¼ cup (60 mL) cinnamon

Glaze
¾ cup (185 mL) brown sugar (3rd amount)
⅓ cup (85 mL) butter

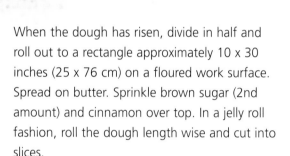

Preheat oven to 350°F (180°C).

In the bowl of an upright electric mixer fitted with the dough hook, add water, ½ cup brown sugar and yeast. Allow the yeast to proof.

Add flour, oil, salt, egg and egg yolk. Mix well. Set aside for about 1 hour in a draft-free place to let the dough rise.

When the dough has risen, divide in half and roll out to a rectangle approximately 10 x 30 inches (25 x 76 cm) on a floured work surface. Spread on butter. Sprinkle brown sugar (2nd amount) and cinnamon over top. In a jelly roll fashion, roll the dough length wise and cut into slices.

To make the glaze, place brown sugar (3rd amount) and butter in the bowl of an electric mixer fitted with the paddle attachment. Beat until light and fluffy. Spread the mixture evenly over the bottom of a baking pan. Place the cinnamon buns in the pan allowing room to rise. Let rest until buns have doubled in size.

Bake 18-20 minutes. Remove from oven and turn over onto a baking pan of equal size to bring the glaze side face up.

Puddings & Custards

Pudding and custard have been transformed into epicurean fare by contemporary chefs. In this section, Bread Pudding shares the applause with Cloudberry Crème Brûlée, and Petit Pot Chocolat can stand beside Blueberry Cobbler as a gourmet delight.

Pumpkin Crème Brûlée

Grandview Resort, Huntsville, ON

The chef at the Grandview Resort makes a sensation of fall using fresh pumpkin, which delivers a more earthy and natural flavour.

2 cups (500 mL) light cream (10%)
5 large egg yolks
½ cup (125 mL) pumpkin purée*
¼ cup (60 mL) granulated sugar
¾ tsp (4 mL) ground cinnamon
pinch each of ground cloves, ground allspice and salt

Brûlée top
½ cup (125 mL) sugar in the raw

* If you do not have fresh pumpkin purée, canned pumpkin pie filling may be substituted, but you may want to adjust the spices, as canned filling generally has added spices.

Preheat oven to 300°F (150°C).

Place the cream in a heavy-bottomed pot and bring to a boil.

In a medium-sized bowl, whisk together the remaining ingredients. Slowly whisk the hot cream into the egg mixture.

Place four 6-oz (190 mL) brûlée ramekins in a roasting pan. Fill the ramekins with the mixture. Fill the roasting pan halfway with hot water. Place in the oven and cook for 20-30 minutes, or until the custard is just set. Carefully remove pan from oven and let the custards cool completely. Refrigerate until cold.

To serve the crème brûlée, sprinkle the tops evenly with sugar in the raw and caramelize the sugar with a kitchen torch. Move the torch swiftly to avoid over-burning the sugar. If you do not have a kitchen torch, you may place the brûlées in the oven and use the broiler to caramelize the sugar.

Espresso Panna Cotta

Las Aguas, Hamilton, ON

Panna cotta, or cooked cream, is a light and creamy dessert that takes little time to prepare.

1 tbsp (15 mL) gelatin powder
1 cup (250 mL) whole milk (3.25%)
3 cups (750 mL) heavy cream (35%)
5 tbsp (75 mL) granulated sugar
3 tbsp (45 mL) instant coffee
pinch of salt
¼ tsp (1 mL) vanilla extract

In a small bowl, dissolve the gelatin with the milk and set aside.

In a medium-sized saucepan with a heavy bottom, bring cream and sugar to a boil. Stir constantly to dissolve all the sugar. Add the coffee and the gelatin-milk mixture. Let the pot come to a simmer and ensure the gelatin has dissolved. Strain the mixture through a fine sieve to avoid any lumps. Once strained, add salt and vanilla and stir.

Pour mixture into six coffee cups. Refrigerate 4-6 hours or until set. To serve the panna cotta, place the cup on a saucer. Top with a dollop of whipped cream, and sprinkle with cinnamon or cocoa powder.

Café Blueberry Cobbler

The Cheesecake Café, Calgary, AB

No summer is complete without a blueberry dessert, and cobbler is a traditional winner.

Filling
½ cup (125 mL) granulated sugar
1 tbsp (15 mL) corn starch
6 cups (1.5 L) blueberries
1 lemon, zest and juice
pinch of salt
1 tsp (5 mL) ground cinnamon

Biscuit topping
1 cup (250 mL) all-purpose flour
2 tbsp (30 mL) corn meal
¼ cup (60 mL) granulated sugar
2 tsp (10 mL) baking powder
¼ tsp (1 mL) baking soda
¼ tsp (1 mL) salt
4 tbsp (60 mL) unsalted butter, melted
⅓ cup (85 mL) buttermilk
½ tsp (2 mL) vanilla

Sprinkle
½ tsp (2 mL) ground cinnamon
2 tbsp (30 mL) granulated sugar
(mixed together)

Preheat oven to 375°F (190°C).

In a large bowl, combine all ingredients for the filling. Mix until all ingredients are covered by the corn starch and sugar. Pour the filling into an 8-inch (20 cm) glass baking dish set on a baking sheet. Place in the oven for 20-25 minutes, or until the filling starts bubbling around the edges. Remove the berry filling from the oven and set aside.

For the biscuit topping, whisk all dry ingredients together in a medium-sized bowl. In a small bowl, mix butter, buttermilk and vanilla together. Mix the wet ingredients into the dry ingredients and stir until just combined.

Spoon eight portions of the biscuit topping onto the blueberry filling and sprinkle with cinnamon sugar. Increase the oven heat to 425°F (220°C). Bake the cobbler for 15-18 minutes until blueberries are bubbling and the biscuit topping is golden brown. Remove from oven and let rest 20 minutes.

Place a biscuit on each plate and spoon warm filling over top.

Petit Pot Chocolat

Gourmandises Avenue Patisserie
Eastern Passage, NS

Gourmandises' silky smooth pots of chocolate
will make you smile.

2 cups (500 mL) whole milk (3.25%)
½ cup (125 mL) granulated sugar
5 large egg yolks
4 oz (120 g) dark chocolate (60%), finely
   chopped
¼ cup (65 mL) hazelnut praline*
2 tbsp (30 mL) pure cocoa liqueur
*Available at most specialty shops. May be
   substituted with peanut butter or Nutella.

In a saucepan with a heavy bottom, bring milk
and half of the sugar to a boil.

In a medium-sized bowl, place the egg yolks,
remaining sugar, chocolate and hazelnut paste.
Slowly pour the hot milk over the mixture and
stir constantly to blend all ingredients together.

Return the mixture to the pot and stir constantly
over medium heat until it begins to thicken.

Remove from heat and add cocoa liqueur. Strain
through a fine mesh sieve to prevent lumps in
the custard. Pour the custard into small coffee
cups and refrigerate until set.

To present the custards, place a dollop of
whipped cream and a sprinkle of instant
espresso powder on top.

Chocolate Obsession with Raspberry Coulis

Sweet Obsessions, Vancouver, BC

This flourless chocolate dessert is light and velvety. The chef at Sweet Obsessions uses a triangular-shaped pan to make this dessert, but a round pan works just as well.

Cake

16 oz (455 g) semi-sweet chocolate, roughly chopped
1 cup (250 mL) unsalted butter, cubed
6 large eggs

Raspberry Coulis

2½-3 pints (680 g) raspberries
2 cups (500 mL) granulated sugar

Preheat oven to 400°F (200°C). Line an 8-inch (20 cm) springform pan with parchment paper.

Set a large bowl over a pot of simmering water. Melt chocolate and butter together, and stir constantly with a wooden spoon. When the chocolate is almost melted, remove the bowl from the pot, and let the residual heat melt the remainder of the chocolate. Cool until tepid.

In the bowl of an electric mixer fitted with whisk attachment, whip eggs until double in volume. Stir in one quarter of the whipped egg to loosen the chocolate. Carefully fold in the remaining eggs and stir.

Pour into the prepared pan and bake in the middle of the oven for 20 minutes. To add moisture and prevent cracks in the cake, place a pan of boiling water on the bottom rack of the oven.

Remove from oven and cool on a wire rack. Place in refrigerator to set. Remove the cake two hours before serving.

To make the coulis, place raspberries and sugar in the bowl of a food processor. Pulse a few times to break down the berries and sugar. Strain the mixture through a fine sieve to remove seeds.

Cut the cake into 12 portions and spoon coulis around the plate. Top with a dollop of whipped cream.

Black Bing Cherry Clafouti

Clafouti, Toronto, ON

The cherries is this dessert can be substituted with other fruit, such as peaches, raspberries, plums or lychees.

1½ cups (375 mL) pitted Bing cherries
2 tbsp (30 mL) butter
½ cup (125 mL) all-purpose flour
½ (125 mL) granulated sugar
¼ cup (60 mL) whole milk (3.25%)
1 tbsp (15 mL) Grand Marnier
1 tbsp (15 mL) Kirsch

Preheat oven to 400°F (200°C). Generously grease a 3-inch (7 cm) ceramic baking dish with butter and place cherries on the bottom.

In a medium-sized bowl, mix flour and sugar together, and make a well in the centre. Place eggs in the well. Slowly mix with a fork while gradually adding milk and liqueur.

Slowly pour the mixture over the cherries. Place in the middle of the oven and bake for 40 minutes or until set and beginning to brown.

To serve the clafouti, spoon portions onto serving plate and sprinkle with confectioner's sugar and a pool of vanilla cream sauce such as crème anglaise.

Cloudberry Crème Brûlée

Bianca's, St. John's, NL

Cloudberries, also known as bake apples, grow in marshy areas and look similar to orange raspberries. In Newfoundland and Cape Breton, they are generally stewed and served with cream. Bianca's transforms them into a heavenly brûlée.

3 cups (750 mL) heavy cream (35%)
2 whole eggs
8 egg yolks
1 cup (250 mL) granulated sugar
1 vanilla bean, seeds only
1½ cups (375 mL) cooked cloudberries
½ tsp (2 mL) ground cinnamon
pinch of nutmeg

Preheat oven to 300°F (150°C).

In a medium-sized saucepan, bring cream to a boil.

In a medium-sized bowl, whisk together eggs, yolks, sugar and vanilla bean seeds. Slowly pour the warmed cream into the egg mixture, followed by the cloudberries and spices.

Pour mixture into 6 6-oz (190 mL) ramekins and place into a roasting pan, filled halfway with hot water. Bake for 60 minutes or until just set. The custards should be a little soft in the centre. Allow the custards to cool until set.

To serve the crème brûlée, sprinkle the tops evenly with sugar in the raw and caramelize the sugar with a kitchen torch. Move the torch swiftly to avoid over-burning the sugar. If you do not have a kitchen torch, you may place the brûlées in the oven and use the broiler to caramelize the sugar.

Caramel Cheese Mousse

Patisserie du Soleil, Calgary, AB

This light cheesecake combines the contrasting textures and flavours of pecans and caramel.

Crust
1½ cups (375 mL) toasted pecans
4 tbsp (60 mL) granulated sugar
¼ cup (60 mL) butter, melted

Mousse
2 tbsp (30 mL) granulated sugar
4¼ cups (1 L) heavy cream (35%)
8-oz package (240 g) cream cheese, room
    temperature
1 tbsp (15 g) water
¼ cup (60 mL) caramel sauce
½ cup (125 mL) caramel fond (or caramel
    pudding)

In the bowl of a food processor fitted with a metal blade, place the pecans in and pulse a few times to coarsely chop the nuts. Pour the chopped pecan pieces into a small bowl and mix in the sugar and melted butter. Press into the bottom of a 10-inch (25 cm) springform pan lined with parchment paper.

For the mousse, whip the cream and sugar to soft peaks in the bowl of an electric mixer. Add the cream cheese and continue to mix for 2-3 minutes, or until just combined.

In a small bowl, mix water, caramel sauce and caramel fond. Add the caramel mixture to the cream cheese batter. Mix until just combined. Pour the caramel cheese mousse over the pecan crust. Cover and refrigerate 6-8 hours or until set.

Remove from the refrigerator and cut into 12 pieces.

In a spiral motion, drizzle some caramel or chocolate sauce over a plate. Place a slice of the mousse in the centre of the plate. Garnish with whipped cream and a sprig of fresh mint.

Kaffir Lime, Ginger and Coconut Custards with Lemongrass Sorbet

Liaison College, Hamilton, ON

Kaffir lime leaves are fragrant and full of flavour. If unavailable, substitute the zest of three limes.

Custard
3 cups (750 mL) heavy cream (35%)
¾ cup (185 mL) coconut milk
5 Kaffir lime leaves
3 tbsp (45 mL) chopped ginger
8 whole eggs
4 egg yolks
1 cup (250 mL) granulated sugar
½ tsp (2 mL) salt

Sorbet
2 lemongrass stalks
1 cup (250 mL) granulated sugar
1 cup (250 mL) water

Macadamia shortbread cookies
¼ cup (60 mL) granulated sugar
½ cup (125 mL) butter
1 cup (250 mL) all-purpose flour
½ cup (125 mL) macadamia nut pieces

Preheat oven to 350°F (180°C). Butter the sides of 12 small ramekins.

In a heavy-bottomed pot, bring cream and coconut milk to a boil. Add lime leaves and chopped ginger. Remove from heat and allow the flavours to steep for 15-20 minutes.

In a mixing bowl, whisk eggs, yolks, sugar and salt together. Slowly pour in cream mixture and stir to combine.

Strain the mixture through a sieve and pour into prepared ramekins. Place ramekins in a roasting pan filled halfway with hot water. Bake for about 15 minutes or until just set. Allow custards to cool before refrigerating.

For the sorbet, pound the lemongrass with the back of a knife and slice into small pieces. Place all ingredients into a pot, and bring to a rolling boil. Remove from heat and allow the sorbet base to cool. Pour the base into an ice cream maker and freeze according to directions. Place finished sorbet in freezer until needed.

For the cookies, preheat oven to 375°F (190°C).

In a medium-sized bowl, cream sugar and butter together using a wooden spoon. Add flour and nuts, and gently knead until a dough is reached. Roll the dough out to ¼-inch (8 mm) thickness and cut out 2-inch (5 cm) discs. Place the cut cookies on a baking sheet and bake for 10-12 minutes or until just turning golden in colour.

To serve, gently run a knife blade around the custard and unmold. Place three custards in the centre of a large plate. Top each custard with a cookie and place a scoop of sorbet in the centres. Dust the plates with icing sugar and garnish with a sprig of lemon balm.

Bread Pudding

Amici, Winnipeg, MB

Comfort foods make one feel at home, and this bread pudding does that very well.

2 baguettes
4 cups (1 L) whole milk (3.25%)
2 cups (500 mL) heavy cream (35%)
8 large egg yolks
4 large eggs
½ cup (125 mL) granulated sugar
1 tbsp (15 mL) vanilla
¼ cup (60 mL) dark rum
¼ cup (60 mL) shaved white chocolate
⅛ cup (30 mL) shaved dark chocolate
1 cup (250 mL) pitted Bing cherries

Preheat oven to 350°F (180°C). Coat 12 6-oz (190 mL) ramekins with non-stick spray. Set aside until needed.

Slice the baguettes into ¼-inch (½ cm) slices.

Place milk, cream, yolks, eggs, sugar, vanilla and rum into a large bowl and whisk until combined. Add the sliced bread, the white and dark chocolate, and cherries.

Layer the bread and cherries in the prepared ramekins, pressing the bread lightly after each layer. When the bread is evenly divided between the ramekins, slowly pour in some of the cream mixture until the bread will no longer absorb any more liquid.

Place the filled ramekin in a roasting pan and fill the pan with hot water until halfway up the sides of the ramekins. Cover with foil and bake for 45 minutes.

Remove from oven and let cool slightly. Unmold the pudding onto plates. Drizzle with caramel sauce or top with whipped cream.

Chocolate Marquis

Patisserie du Soleil, Calgary, AB

The combination of milk and semi-sweet chocolate gives new life to this velvety, rich classic.

19 oz (535 g) semi-sweet chocolate, chopped
19 oz (535 g) milk chocolate, chopped
2½ cups (625 mL) butter
10 large egg whites, room temperature
1½ cups (375 mL) granulated sugar
1¾ cup (430 mL) strong coffee, warm
¾ cup (185 mL) cocoa powder
1 store-bought 8-inch (20 cm) white cake

Line the sides of 10-inch (25 cm) springform pan with parchment paper. Place a layer of white cake on the bottom of the pan.

Place the semi-sweet and milk chocolate in a large glass bowl with the butter. Set the bowl over a pot of simmering water to melt the chocolate and butter. Once the chocolate is almost melted, remove the bowl from the pot and allow to cool.

Place the egg whites in the bowl of an electric mixer and whisk until soft peaks are formed. Gradually add the sugar and continue to whisk until firm peaks. Set aside.

Pour the coffee and cocoa powder into the cooled chocolate. Stir to combine. Gently cut and fold the chocolate mixture into the meringue. Mix until just combined. Pour mixture into prepared pan. Place the pan in the refrigerator for 6 hours to let set.

Gently loosen the sides of the springform pan and remove the cake. Cut the cake into 16 pieces. Garnish with whipped cream and instant coffee granules.

Tarts

Pastry is a cook's best friend. It makes possible a wide variety of baked desserts, clever combinations and artistic presentations. This section opens up a world of tempting tarts, from Tarte Aux Poires au Chocolat (Chocolate Pear Tart) to Crisp Cashew Tarts with White Chocolate Truffle Cream and Lime Curd. The zing of Ginger Lemon Tart and the sensual contrasts in Chocolate Raspberry Flan will keep dessert lovers coming back for more.

Apple Cranberry Tart

True Confections, Vancouver, BC

In this dessert, the flavours of autumn are served warm with cool vanilla gelato.

Tart dough

1½ cups (375 mL) all-purpose flour
6 tbsp (90 mL) granulated sugar
1 cup (250 mL) unsalted butter, cold and cut into pieces
3 large egg yolks
¼ tsp (1 mL) salt
½ tsp (2 mL) vanilla extract

Filling

1½ lbs (680 g) favourite apples, peeled and quartered
2¼ cups (560 mL) fresh cranberries
6 tbsp (90 mL) granulated sugar
2 tbsp (30 mL) all-purpose flour

Streusel topping

¼ cup (60 mL) brown sugar
¼ cup (60 mL) pecans, toasted and chopped
6 tbsp (90 mL) all-purpose flour
4 tbsp (60 mL) unsalted butter, cut into small pieces
1 tbsp (15 mL) granulated sugar
1 tsp (5 mL) vanilla extract
pinch of salt

To make the tart dough, place all ingredients in the bowl of a food processor fitted with a metal blade. Pulse until the dough forms a ball. Remove dough and shape into a flat disc. Wrap with plastic wrap and refrigerate at least one hour.

Mix all ingredients for the filling in a medium-sized bowl. Set aside until needed.

Mix all ingredients for the streusel in another bowl and set aside.

Preheat oven to 350°F (180°C).

Remove tart dough from the fridge. Roll out dough to ⅛ inch (8 mm) in thickness. Line an 11-inch (28 cm) tart pan with a removable bottom with the dough. Using a fork, poke holes in the dough and freeze for 15-20 minutes.

Remove from freezer and bake for 10-15 minutes. Remove from oven and let cool slightly.

Place the apple cranberry filling in the crust. Bake for 30-35 minutes.

Remove from oven and top with streusel mix. Place back in oven and continue to cook for 25 minutes. Remove from oven and let cool on a wire rack.

Once the tart has cooled, cut into 12 portions. Serve warm or cold, with whipped cream or gelato.

Ginger Lemon Tart

Kinki's, Ottawa, ON

The ginger in this tart adds a bit of spice to the traditional lemon tart.

Crust
1 cup (250 mL) graham wafer crumbs
½ cup (125 mL) granulated sugar
6 tbsp (90 mL) butter, melted

Filling
8 lemons, juiced
1¼ cup (215 mL) granulated sugar
12 egg yolks
1½ tbsp (25 mL) fresh ginger, grated
1½ cups (375 mL) butter

Preheat oven to 375°F (190°C).

In a bowl, combine the graham wafer crumbs, sugar and melted butter and press firmly into the bottom of a 10-inch (25 cm) springform pan. Place in oven and bake for 5-7 minutes.

Set a medium-sized glass bowl over a pot of simmering water. Combine the lemon juice, sugar, egg yolks and grated ginger. Whisk constantly for about 10 minutes, or until a thick custard is reached. Remove bowl from simmering water and whisk in butter.

Strain mixture through a fine sieve into the pre-baked graham wafer bottom. Cover with plastic wrap. Poke a few holes in the plastic wrap to vent any steam. Place in refrigerator overnight.

When cooled, run a sharp knife around the pan to loosen the tart. Open springform and gently remove.

Torta di Ricotta

Prairie Ink Restaurant and Bakery, Saskatoon, SK

This traditional Italian cheesecake uses Ricotta cheese, giving it Sicilian roots.

16-oz tub (455 g) ricotta cheese
2 oz (60 g) semi-sweet chocolate, roughly
  chopped into small pieces
¾ cup (185 mL) granulated sugar
1 tbsp (15 mL) orange liqueur
1 tbsp (15 mL) vanilla
2 eggs
2 egg yolks
1 pre-made pie shell
½ cup (125 mL) toasted sliced almonds
Marsala wine (optional)
¼ cup (125 mL) ground espresso

Preheat oven to 325°F (160°C).

In a large mixing bowl, whisk the ricotta cheese until creamy. Add the chopped chocolate, sugar, orange liqueur, vanilla, eggs and egg yolks, mixing until well incorporated.

Pour the mixture into the pie shell and bake for 25-30 minutes or until firm to the touch. Remove from oven and let cool.

To present this dessert, pour 2 tbsp (30 mL) of Marsala wine on each serving plate. Place a wedge of torta on the plate, and sprinkle with almonds and espresso.

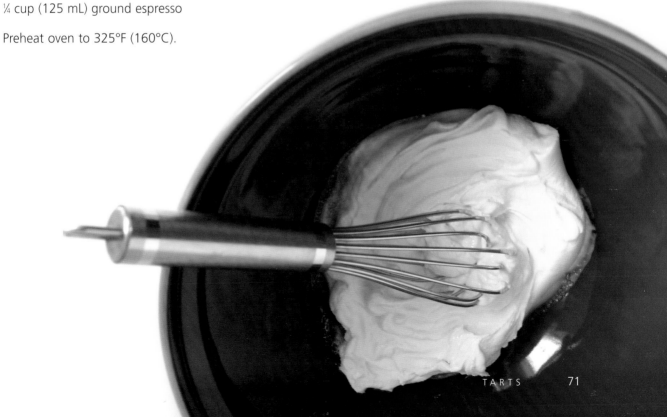

Lemon Brûlée Tart

Room For Dessert, Dundas, ON

The tangy lemon in this tart is softened by the brûlée crunch.

Pastry
1½ cups (375 mL) all-purpose flour
¼ cup (60 mL) granulated sugar
¾ cup (190 mL) butter, cold and cubed into
    rough pieces
1 tbsp (15 mL) white vinegar

Filling
3 large eggs
1½ cups (375 mL) granulated sugar
1 tbsp (15 mL) grated lemon zest
½ cup (125 mL) lemon juice (approximately 4
    lemons)
½ cup (125 mL) all-purpose flour

Brûlée topping
½ cup (125 mL) raw sugar

White chocolate cream
4 oz (120 g) white chocolate
1½ cups (375 mL) heavy cream (35 %)

Preheat oven to 375°F (170°C).

In the basket of a food processor, combine the flour, sugar and butter. Pulse until the mixture resembles a fine meal. Add the vinegar and process again until the dough just comes together.

Remove the dough from the food processor and form into a disc shape. Wrap with plastic wrap and let rest in the fridge for 30 minutes.

Once the dough has rested, roll out enough to line a 9-inch (23 cm) tart pan with a removable bottom. Let the lined tart pan sit in the freezer for 45 minutes.

To make the filling, whisk all the ingredients together in a large bowl.

Remove the pastry from the freezer and pour in the filling. Bake for 20-30 minutes or until the filling is set and the pastry is golden. Remove the tart from the oven and let cool.

Transfer the tart from the pan to a serving plate and sprinkle raw sugar evenly over the entire surface. With a blowtorch, begin to brûlée the top by melting and browning the sugar.

For the white chocolate cream, melt the chocolate in a small saucepan. Add cream and stir, or remove chocolate from heat and place in bowl of an electric mixer. Add cream and whip until thick

Cut the tart into eight pieces and serve with the white chocolate cream.

Chocolate Banana Tart

Diva at the Met, Vancouver, BC

Working with phyllo pastry takes a little practice, but the results are always pleasing.

Tart shells
5 sheets of phyllo pastry
¼ cup (60 mL) butter, melted
icing sugar

Banana filling
3 large bananas
1 tbsp (15 mL) lemon juice
4 tbsp (60 mL) granulated sugar
2 tbsp (30 mL) unsalted butter
2 tbsp (30 mL) dark rum

Chocolate ganache
¾ cup (190 mL) heavy cream (35%)
4 tsp (20 mL) liquid honey
4 oz (120 g) semi-sweet chocolate, chopped
    finely

Preheat oven to 350°F (180°C).

To make the phyllo tart shell, lay one sheet of phyllo on counter. Working quickly, brush with melted butter and dust with icing sugar. Lay another sheet of phyllo on top. Brush with melted butter and dust with icing sugar. Repeat with each layer, ending with a plain layer of phyllo.

With a rolling pin, gently roll over top ensuring the layers stick together. Brush with melted butter. With a sharp knife, cut out four circles 7 inches (15 cm) in diameter. Line 4 buttered foil tart pans with the phyllo layers. Place another 4-inch (10 cm) foil tart pan filled with beans onto each. Place on a baking sheet, and bake for 12 minutes. Remove the bean-filled tart pans and continue to cook for another 3 minutes, or until golden brown. Remove from oven and let cool.

Cut bananas into ½-inch (1 cm) long pieces and toss in a bowl. Add lemon juice.

Heat a large skillet over medium heat and add sugar. When sugar begins to take on an amber colour, stir in butter and add bananas. Toss and stir to coat bananas in the caramel for 2 minutes. Remove pan from heat and stir in rum. Set aside.

For the ganache, bring heavy cream and honey to a boil. Add chocolate and stir until smooth. Remove from heat.

To assemble the tarts, spoon enough banana mixture to fill ¼ of the tart shell. Pour ganache into shells to cover the bananas. Refrigerate for 20 minutes or until chocolate is set. Remove from the refrigerator and let come to room temperature before serving.

Serve with your favourite gelato.

Crisp Cashew Tarts with White Chocolate Truffle Cream and Lime Curd

Dufflet Pastries, Toronto, ON

The combination of white chocolate, lime and cashews in this dessert creates an extraordinary balance of flavours.

Lime curd
2 large eggs
2 large yolks
½ cup (125 mL) granulated sugar
6 tbsp (90 mL) lime juice
2 tsp (10 mL) lime zest
½ cup (125 mL) unsalted butter, cold and cubed

Passion fruit crème anglaise
1 cup (250 mL) passion fruit juice
1 cup (250 mL) heavy cream (35%)
4 large egg yolks
¼ cup (60 mL) granulated sugar

White chocolate truffle cream
12 oz (360 g) white chocolate, chopped finely
½ cup (125 mL) heavy cream (35%)
1½ cup (275 mL) heavy cream (35%)

Tart shells
5 sheets of phyllo pastry
6 tbsp (90 mL) melted butter
⅓ cup (85 mL) cashew pieces

Garnish
zest of 2 limes
½ cup (125 mL) toasted cashews
2 passion fruits

To make the lime curd, place all ingredients in a heavy-bottomed, non-reactive pot. Place over medium heat and stir constantly with a wooden spoon until thick. Remove from heat. Pour into a container and place plastic wrap directly on the surface to prevent a skin from forming. Place in refrigerator to cool.

To make the passion fruit crème anglaise, bring the passion fruit juice to a boil. Reduce heat by half. In a separate saucepan, bring the cream to a boil and then add the fruit juice. Remove from heat.

In a medium-sized bowl, whisk yolks and sugar until pale in colour. Slowly pour a little cream mixture in with yolks and sugar. Pour the yolk mixture into the cream and continue to cook over medium heat. Stir constantly with a wooden spoon until it coats the back of the spoon. Remove from heat and strain into a bowl. Cover with plastic wrap directly on the surface. Refrigerate until needed.

To make the truffle cream, place the chocolate in a medium-sized bowl. Bring ½ cup (125 mL) of cream to a boil and pour over the chocolate. Stir until smooth. Cool in the freezer for about 5 minutes.

While the chocolate is cooling, whip the remaining 1½ cups (375 mL) cream to medium firm peaks. Remove the cooled chocolate from the freezer and stir in ⅓ of the whipped cream. Fold in remaining cream and place in fridge to set.

Preheat oven to 375°F (190°C). Working quickly with the phyllo, take one sheet and brush with melted butter. Place second sheet on top, brush with butter and sprinkle with ⅓ of the cashews. Continue the same process with third and forth sheets. Top with the fifth sheet and roll over the phyllo with a rolling pin to ensure each layer is secure. With a sharp paring knife, cut 6 circles about 4 inches (10 cm) in diameter. Brush the tops with butter.

Line 6 tart pans with the phyllo layers. Bake for 6-7 minutes or until golden brown. Remove from oven and let cool on a wire rack.

To assemble and serve, spread 2 tbsp (30 mL) lime curd in each tart shell. Fill a pastry bag with truffle cream and pipe in a spiral fashion to fill the shell. Place one tart on each plate and drizzle crème anglaise around tart. Cut the passion fruits in half and spoon a little around the plate. Top with lime zest and sprinkle with cashews.

Milk Chocolate Chai-Spice Tart

Queen of Tarts, Toronto, ON

The combination of chai and chocolate brings an eastern flavour to this elegant tart.

Crust
2 cups (500 mL) all-purpose flour
½ cup (125 mL) granulated sugar
½ cup (125 mL) cocoa powder
1 cup (250 mL) unsalted butter
2 large egg yolks
2 tbsp (30 mL) heavy cream (35%)

Chocolate-Chai Filling
16 oz (455 g) milk chocolate, finely chopped
½ cup (125 mL) heavy cream (35%)
1 tbsp (15 mL) loose chai

In the bowl of an electric mixer fitted with the paddle attachment, on low speed, mix all dry ingredients with butter until pea-size.

In a small bowl, whisk together yolks and cream. Pour into the flour-butter mixture and continue on low speed until just combined.

Remove dough from bowl and knead lightly on a floured surface until smooth. Flatten into a round disc, wrap with plastic wrap and let rest in refrigerator overnight.

Roll dough out to ⅛ inch (8 mm) in thickness and line an 11-inch (28 cm) tart pan with a removable bottom. Chill the tart crust for 4 hours in the refrigerator.

Preheat oven to 350°F (180°C). Line the tart crust with parchment paper and fill with pie weights. Bake blind for 10-12 minutes. Remove the parchment and weights, and continue to bake for 5-10 minutes, or until the crust is golden brown. Remove from oven and let cool on a wire rack.

When crust is cool, carefully remove from the pan.

For the filling, bring cream and chai spice to a boil in a heavy-bottomed saucepan. Remove from heat, cover and let steep for 20-30 minutes.

Place chocolate in a medium-sized bowl. Bring the cream-chai mixture back to a boil. Strain over the chocolate. With a whisk, stir until smooth. Pour into tart crust and refrigerate for 3 hours or until set.

To serve, cut tart into 12 pieces. Spoon a dollop of whipped cream on each slice and sprinkle with cinnamon.

Chocolate Raspberry Flan

Fleurdelys Patisserie, Toronto, ON

The addition of fresh, tart raspberries to this rich chocolate tart makes this dessert irresistible.

Crust
4 cups (1000 mL) all-purpose flour
¾ cup (200 mL) granulated sugar
2¼ cups (560 mL) unsalted butter, cold
2 large eggs
3 large egg yolks

Filling
17½ oz (510 g) semi-sweet chocolate, chopped
2 cups (500 mL) heavy cream (35%)
7 tbsp (100 mL) unsalted butter
2 cups (500 mL) fresh raspberries

Preheat oven to 375°F (190°C).

In the bowl of a food processor fitted with a metal blade, combine flour, sugar and butter. Pulse until pieces are pea-size. Add eggs and yolks. Pulse until the dough just comes together.

Remove dough and flatten into a round disc. Cover with plastic wrap and refrigerate for 45 minutes.

Roll the dough to ⅛ inch (8 mm) in thickness. Using this dough, line an 11-inch (28 cm) tart pan with a removable bottom. Place the crust in the freezer for 30 minutes to rest. Bake the crust for 15 minutes or until golden brown. Remove from oven and let cool completely on a wire rack.

To make the filling, place the chopped chocolate in a medium-sized bowl. Pour the cream into a heavy-bottomed saucepan and bring to a boil. Pour the hot cream over the chocolate. Add butter and stir with a wooden spoon until smooth.

Pour the filling into the cooled crust and top with fresh raspberries. Place in the fridge for 4-5 hours or overnight.

Cut tart into 12 pieces. Serve with whipped cream.

Tarte aux Poires et Chocolat

Julien's Bakery and Café, Halifax, NS

The flavours of Normandy are infused into this pear tart.

Crust
½ cup (125 mL) all-purpose flour
3½ tbsp (50 mL) granulated sugar
½ tsp (2 mL) salt
½ cup (125 mL) unsalted butter, cubed
3½ tbsp (50 mL) ice cold water
1 egg yolk

Filling
4½ oz (120 g) semi-sweet chocolate, finely
  chopped
3 ripe pears
1 tbsp (15 mL) granulated sugar

Custard
1 egg
1 egg yolk
½ cup (125 mL) heavy cream (35%)
1 tsp (5 mL) vanilla extract

Preheat oven to 375°F (190°C).

To make the crust, combine flour, sugar, and salt in a large bowl. Cut in butter with a pastry blender or two knives. Add yolk and mix with a fork until just combined. Remove dough from bowl and flatten into a round disc. Cover with plastic wrap and let rest in the refrigerator for 30 minutes. Remove and roll out to ⅛ inch (8 mm) in thickness and place in an 11-inch (28 cm) tart pan with removable bottom. Let rest in refrigerator for 1 hour.

Remove tart pan from the refrigerator and poke holes in the bottom with a fork. Line with foil wrap and fill with pie weights. Bake blind for 20 minutes. Remove the foil and weights, and continue to bake for 10 minutes or until golden brown. Remove from oven and let cool on a wire rack.

When crust has cooled, sprinkle the bottom with chocolate. Peel and core the pears. Thinly slice the pears crosswise. Place the pear pieces on top of the chocolate with the tips of the pears facing inward.

To make the custard, place all ingredients in a medium-sized bowl and whisk until pale in colour. Pour the custard over the pears and sprinkle with sugar. Bake for 40 minutes or until pears are tender and the custard is set and golden brown. Remove from oven and let cool on a wire rack.

Warm Apple Tart

Boulangerie la Vendienne, Mahone Bay, NS

With the addition of Calvados (apple brandy), you have a dessert straight from northern France.

10 McIntosh apples
½ cup + 2 tbsp (155 mL) granulated sugar
3½ tbsp (50 mL) water
1 rosemary sprig
11-oz package (330 g) puff pastry
1 tbsp (15 mL) unsalted butter
6 tbsp (90 mL) Calvados
crème fraîche

Peel, core and slice six of the apples. Place apples in a 10-inch (25 cm) oven-proof skillet with 4 tbsp (60 mL) of sugar, water and rosemary. Cook over medium-low heat until tender and roughly mash the apples so you have a chunky sauce. Remove from heat and let cool.

Roll the puff pastry into a circle about ¼ inch (16 mm) in thickness and place on a baking sheet. Poke holes in the pastry with a fork and spread the cooled applesauce over top.

Peel, core and slice the remaining four apples and fan over the top. Sprinkle 2 tbsp (30 mL) of sugar over top and bake for 10-15 minutes, or until the top is browned.

Just before serving, place the Calvados in a pot and heat gently. Ignite and pour over the tart. Serve with a dollop of crème fraîche.

Apple Tart Tatin with Heavy Cream

Liaison College, Hamilton, ON

This classic French apple tart brings warm feelings of autumn to mind.

2 tbsp (30 mL) unsalted butter
½ cup (125 mL) granulated sugar
1 tbsp (15 mL) lemon juice
2 lbs (900 g) cooking apples, cored, peeled and
  halved
11-oz package (330 g) prepared puff pastry
½ cup (125 mL) heavy cream (35%)
½ cup (125 mL) icing sugar
1 tbsp (15 mL) vanilla

Preheat oven to 425°F (220°C).

In a 10-inch (25 cm) oven-proof skillet with high sides, melt butter over medium heat. Add sugar and lemon juice, and stir until combined. Place the apple halves upright around the side of the skillet until the skillet is completely full. If there are any spaces, cut the apples to fill holes. Continue to cook the apples over medium heat for about 25 minutes, or until the sugar begins bubbling around the apples and is amber in colour.

Place the skillet in the oven for 5 minutes.

On a lightly floured surface, roll the puff pastry out to ¼ inch (16 mm) in thickness. Remove the apples from the oven and increase heat to 475°F (245°C). Drape the pastry over the apples and, using a small palate knife, tuck the pastry around the inside of the skillet. Place the skillet in the oven and bake for 15-20 minutes, or until pastry is lightly brown. Remove from oven and let cool slightly on a wire rack.

When the tart has cooled slightly, place a serving plate over the skillet and turn the tart on to the plate. Straighten any apples that may have come out.

Place cream, sugar and vanilla in a chilled bowl and whip until soft peaks.

Cut the tart into 8 pieces and serve with whipped cream.

Milk Chocolate Caramel Tarts

Dufflet Pastries, Toronto, ON

This rich milk chocolate tart is balanced with the sweet flavour of caramel.

Cocoa tart pastry

2½ cups (625 mL) all-purpose flour
1½ cups (375 mL) icing sugar
½ cup (125 mL) cocoa powder
1 cup (250 mL) unsalted butter, chilled and cut
  into pieces
2 large eggs

Caramel sauce

1 cup (250 mL) heavy cream (35%)
1¾ cups (440 mL) granulated sugar
5 tbsp (75 mL) unsalted butter
1 tsp (5 mL) pure vanilla extract

Milk chocolate filling

1 lb (455 g) milk chocolate, cut into small pieces
1½ cups (375 mL) heavy cream (35%)
1½ tbsp (23 mL) unsalted butter

Preheat oven to 375°F (190°C).

In the bowl of a food processor, combine flour, sugar, cocoa and butter until it resembles course meal. Add eggs and process until just combined.

Remove dough from the bowl and gently knead until smooth. Divide the dough in half and flatten into discs. Wrap with plastic wrap and chill for 30 minutes.

Roll the dough out to ⅛ inch (8 mm) in thickness. Cut 4-inch (10 cm) circles out of the dough using a biscuit cutter. Line 12 3½-inch (9 cm) tart pans with the circles, making sure to pinch the dough up the sides and poke the shells with a fork. Place the prepared tart pans on a baking sheet and chill until firm.

Remove the tart shells from the fridge and place directly into the oven. Bake for 10-12 minutes or until the shells are golden in colour. Remove from oven and cool on a wire rack.

To make the caramel sauce, place the cream, sugar and butter into a heavy-bottomed saucepan. Cook over medium-high heat until the mixture is a rich amber colour. Remove from the heat and let cool. Once the sauce has cooled, stir in the vanilla. If you find the sauce thickens too much, heat some cream and pour it into the sauce to loosen.

For the milk chocolate filling, place chocolate into a medium-sized bowl. Bring 1 cup (250 mL) of cream to a boil and pour over the chocolate. Let the cream and chocolate sit for a moment. Add butter and begin to whisk until fully incorporated. Let cool slightly. Whip the remainder of cream in a bowl. When the chocolate mixture has cooled slightly, fold the whipped cream into the chocolate.

Remove the tart shells from the pans and fill with the chocolate mixture. Place the tart pans on a baking sheet and tap gently on work surface to allow any air to come to the surface. Place in refrigerator to set. Bring to room temperature before serving.

To present the tart, dust the tops with cocoa. Warm the caramel sauce slightly and drizzle over plates in spiral motion. Place a tart in the centre of the plate and garnish with fresh berries.

Truffles

Truffles are elegant nuggets of chocolate that get their name from another delicacy — a fungi that grows underground and has been enjoyed in Europe since Roman times as an aphrodisiac and as medicine. The chocolate truffles in this section are hand-made temptations that may well have some of the properties of their namesake.

Duo of Chocolate

Las Aguas, Hamilton, ON

This dessert will surely please the palates of your next dinner guests. You may serve the soufflé and pâté separately or together.

Chocolate pâté

1 lb (455 g) semi-sweet chocolate, finely
    chopped
12 tbsp (180 mL) unsalted butter
¾ cup (185 mL) heavy cream (35%)
2 tbsp (30 mL) orange liqueur
2 egg yolks

Chocolate soufflé

6 tbsp (90 mL) unsalted butter
6 tbsp (90 mL) all-purpose flour
2 cups (500 mL) whole milk (3.25%)
½ cup (125 mL) granulated sugar
8 oz (240 g) semi-sweet chocolate, finely
    chopped
1 tbsp (15 mL) vanilla
8 eggs, separated
¼ cup (65 mL) granulated sugar

This dessert requires two days to prepare, but only 30 minutes for each part, plus cooling time. The soufflés can be made ahead of time, to the point of the addition of the whites. Prepare the base, and let sit at room temperature until needed. The pâté can also be pre-sliced and ready to plate.

Day one: Line a small loaf pan with plastic wrap. To make the pâté, place the chocolate in a medium-sized bowl. Bring butter and cream to a boil in a small saucepan. Pour over the chocolate and stir with a wooden spoon until smooth. Stir in egg yolks and orange liqueur. Pour into prepared loaf pan and refrigerate overnight.

Day two: Preheat oven to 375°F (190°C).

Prepare 10 2-oz (65 mL) soufflé dishes by generously buttering and dusting the dishes with granulated sugar. Set aside.

In a medium-sized bowl, mix butter and flour to form a smooth paste.

In a medium-sized saucepan, bring milk and sugar to a boil. Slowly whisk into the flour mixture, making sure there are no lumps.

Return the mixture to the saucepan and bring back to a boil, stirring constantly with a wooden spoon. Remove from heat and add the chocolate, stirring until melted. Pour into a medium-sized bowl and let cool slightly.

Whip egg whites to firm peaks in a clean grease-free bowl with an electric mixer. Stir yolks and vanilla into the chocolate base until just mixed. Stir a little of the whites into the base to loosen the batter, and gently fold in the remaining whites.

Pour into prepared soufflé dishes and place on a baking sheet. Place on the middle rack of the oven and bake for 11 minutes. Remove from oven and serve immediately.

For presentation, place two thin slices of pâté on each plate, a soufflé dusted with icing sugar, and some fresh berries.

Cranberry and Coriander Infused Truffles

JS Bonbons, Toronto, ON

The flavour of these truffles is very unique and well worth the effort.

2 cups (500 mL) fresh cranberries
½ cup (125 mL) granulated sugar
17 oz (500 g) milk chocolate, best quality
½ cup (125 mL) heavy cream (35%)
2 tsp (10 mL) ground coriander
4 tbsp (60 mL) unsalted butter
17 oz (500 g) milk chocolate (for enrobing)

Day one: Cook cranberries and sugar in enough water to cover the bottom of the saucepan over medium-high heat until skins burst. Remove pan from heat and let cool. Purée cranberries in a food processor and strain through a mesh strainer.

Roughly chop chocolate into small pieces and place in a medium-sized bowl.

In a clean saucepan, mix heavy cream with cranberry purée and bring just to a boil. In a large bowl, combine chocolate, coriander and butter. Slowly pour hot cream over chocolate mixture, then stir chocolate into cream until all is melted.

Place truffle mixture in a container and refrigerate overnight.

Day two: Remove truffle mixture from the refrigerator. Using your hands, form bite-sized balls and place them on a pan lined with parchment paper.

To enrobe truffle centres, temper the chocolate by roughly chopping it and placing it in a glass bowl set over a pot of simmering water. Make sure the water does not touch the bottom of the bowl. Constantly stir chocolate until almost melted. Remove from heat and allow to cool, stirring occasionally. When chocolate begins to thicken, place the bowl over the simmering water to re-heat slightly. Remove from heat, and enrobe the centres in chocolate. Place truffles on parchment paper. Chocolate should begin to dry and harden in 5 minutes. If not, place truffles in the refrigerator until dry.

Irish Cream Truffles

Gleneagle Bakery, Dartmouth, NS

For the best truffles you need to use the best-quality chocolate, such as Callebaut, Cocoa Barry or Lindt.

1 cup (250 mL) heavy cream (35%)
20 oz (600 g) milk chocolate, finely chopped
4 tbsp (60 mL) unsalted butter
6 tbsp (90 mL) Irish Cream liqueur
2 lbs (1 kg) white chocolate, roughly chopped
  (for enrobing)

This can be used as a base recipe, and you may substitute your favourite liqueur in place of Irish Cream.

Day one: in a small saucepan, bring the cream to a boil.

Place the milk chocolate, butter and liqueur into a medium-sized bowl. When the cream has boiled, slowly pour over the chocolate. Gently stir with a heavy whisk, and continue until smooth. Cover with plastic wrap and refrigerate overnight.

Day two: Remove the chocolate mixture from the refrigerator and, either by hand or using a small portion scoop, make little balls and place them on a baking sheet lined with parchment paper. Set aside.

To temper the enrobing chocolate for the centres, place the white chocolate in a glass bowl and set over a saucepan of simmering water. Make sure the bottom does not touch the water and avoid any contact with steam, as this will make the chocolate seize. Stir the chocolate constantly until almost completely melted. Remove the bowl from the saucepan, and allow the residual heat to melt the remaining chocolate. When the chocolate begins to cool, stir every so often until it becomes thicker and loses its shine. At this point, place the bowl over the simmering water again and stir constantly until just fluid. Remove from heat.

Working with your fingers only, dip each centre in the white chocolate. Roll them around on your fingers to ensure they are totally covered. Place the covered truffles on a clean baking sheet lined with parchment paper. The appearance will be rustic, like little snowballs. However, if you prefer a smooth finish, re-dip truffles using a dipping fork.

When the truffles are dry, store in an airtight container for up to two weeks.

Raspberry Truffles

Gleneagle Bakery, Dartmouth, NS

Once you have mastered these raspberry truffles, you can begin experimenting with other flavours that lend themselves well to combining with chocolate.

1¾ cups (440 mL) heavy cream (35%)
1 lb (455 g) semi-sweet chocolate, finely
  chopped
2 tbsp (30 mL) raspberry liqueur
4 tbsp (60 mL) raspberry preserves
1½ lbs (680 g) semi-sweet chocolate (for
  enrobing)

Day one: In a small saucepan, bring cream to a boil. Place the chocolate into a medium-sized bowl. Slowly pour the hot cream over the chocolate. Gently stir with a heavy whisk, and continue until smooth. Add raspberry liqueur and preserves, stirring until combined. Cover with plastic wrap and refrigerate overnight.

Day two: Remove the chocolate mixture from the refrigerator and, either by hand or using a small portion scoop, make truffle centres. Place them on a baking sheet lined with parchment paper. Set aside.

To temper the enrobing chocolate for the centres, place the chocolate in a glass bowl and set over a pot of simmering water. Make sure the bottom does not touch the water and avoid any contact with steam, as this will make the chocolate seize. Stir the chocolate constantly until almost completely melted. Remove the bowl from the pot, and allow the residual heat to melt the remaining chocolate. When the chocolate begins to cool, stir every so often until it becomes thicker and loses its shine. At this point, place the bowl over the simmering water again and stir constantly until just fluid. Remove from heat.

Working with your fingers only, dip each centre in the chocolate. Roll them around on your fingers to ensure they are totally covered. Place the covered truffles on a clean baking sheet lined with parchment paper. The appearance will be rustic. If you prefer a smooth finish, re-dip truffles using a dipping fork.

When the truffles are dry, store in an airtight container for up to two weeks.

Index

Acknowledgements

The collection of recipes for this volume was done over the past two years. In that time, of course, people have moved on and establishments have varied their offerings. We would like to thank the chefs and the owners of the following fine patisseries, cafés, bakeries and restaurants for sharing their recipes with us for this project.

Calgary, AB
Cheesecake Café
Patisserie du Soleil

Dartmouth, NS
Gleneagle Bakery

Dundas, ON
Room for Dessert

Eastern Passage, NS
Gourmandises
Avenue Patisserie

Fredericton, NB
Happy Baker

Guelph, ON
With the Grain

Halifax, NS
Gingerbread Haus
Bakery
Julien's Bakery and
Café
La Cave
Seven Restaurant &
Wine Bar

Hamilton, ON
Las Aguas
Liaison College

Huntsville, ON
Grandview Resort

LaHave, NS
LaHave Bakery

London, ON
Braywick Bistro
Café Europa
Elegant Epicure

Mahone Bay, NS
Boulangerie la
Vendienne

Ottawa, ON
Kinki's
Thyme and Again
Creative Catering

Saskatoon, SK
Prairie Ink Restaurant
and Bakery

St. John's, NL
Bianca's

Toronto, ON
Clafouti
Cupcake Shoppe
Dufflet Pastries
Fleurdelys Patisserie
JS Bonbons
Queen of Tarts
Vienna Home Bakery

Vancouver, BC
Diva at the Met
La Baguette et
L'Echalote
Purdy's Chocolates
Senses Bakery
Sweet Obsessions
True Confections

Victoria, BC
Café Brio
Herald Street Café

Winnipeg, MB
Amici
Tall Grass Prairie
Bakery